THE **MINI** ROUGH GUIDE TO
BUDAPEST

YOUR TAILOR-MADE TRIP
STARTS HERE

Tailor-made trips and unique adventures crafted by local experts

HOW ROUGHGUIDES.COM/TRIPS WORKS

STEP 1

Pick your dream destination, tell us what you want and submit an enquiry.

STEP 2

Fill in a short form to tell your local expert about your dream trip and preferences.

STEP 3

Our local expert will craft your tailor-made itinerary. You'll be able to tweak and refine it until you're completely satisfied.

STEP 4

Book online with ease, pack your bags and enjoy the trip! Our local expert will be on hand 24/7 while you're on the road.

PLAN AND BOOK YOUR TRIP AT
ROUGHGUIDES.COM/TRIPS

HOW TO DOWNLOAD YOUR FREE EBOOK

1. Visit **www.roughguides.com/free-ebook** or scan the **QR code** opposite

2. Enter the code **budapest660**

3. Follow the simple step-by-step instructions

For troubleshooting contact: mail@roughguides.com

10 THINGS NOT TO MISS

9am

Breakfast. Have breakfast in the old-fashioned ambience and warm glow of the *Centrál Kávéház* at Károlyi Mihály utca 9 in Pest's Belváros or 'Inner City'.

10am

Hungarian National Museum. Walk a couple of blocks east to Múzeum körút to find the Hungarian National Museum. Take a quick tour of the nation's history, marvelling at exhibits of the Avars' gold jewellery, St Stephen's coronation mantle and communist propaganda posters.

11am

Food Market. Follow the Belváros ringroad south to the vast Central Market Hall, built by Gustave Eiffel, of Eiffel Tower fame. Only the freshest produce is on sale here.

11.30am

Shopping on Váci utca. Cross the road and stroll up the city's premier shopping street. Keep your eyes peeled for handicrafts emporium, Folkart Centrum, which stocks a selection of handmade Hungarian delights, and the magical window displays of florist Philanthia. Emerging in Vörösmarty tér at the end, you will find a stylish shopping centre on your left.

1pm

Gerbeaud. Take a light lunch at this café institution on the far side of Vörösmarty tér. Sit in the grand interior, with its chandeliers and fine plasterwork, or lounge on the terrace for some top-quality people-watching. Save room for one of *Gerbeaud*'s cakes, as these are the café's speciality.

IN **BUDAPEST**

2.15pm

Great square. Take the metro direct from Vörösmarty tér to Heroes' Square at the head of Andrássy út and at the gates of City Park. In the centre of the square is the Millennium Monument, crowned by the Archangel Gabriel. Flanking the square are the Museum of Fine Arts and the Palace of Art.

2.30pm

City Park. Entering City Park, you will be faced with a wide choice of amusing diversions; you could pay a visit to the zoo, extravagantly designed in Art Nouveau style, and see the huge, light-flooded Palm House or be wowed by a riotous two-and-a-half-hour show featuring clowns, acrobats and jugglers at the Capital Circus at 3pm on Wednesday to Sunday (also at 11am on Saturday, Sunday and some Fridays).

5pm

Széchenyi Baths. Also within City Park is the iconic neo-Baroque complex of the Széchenyi Baths. Relax in the balmy pools, indoor and outdoor, play a game of chess with the elderly locals in the shallows or treat yourself to a massage. Afterwards, drink a glass of the health-giving waters at the little pavilion just outside.

7pm

Dinner and a show. Feeling fully rested, it's time to take an easy stroll to *Gundel*, Hungary's most famous restaurant, on the eastern edge of the park, where you can dine in style. Alternatively, take the metro a few stops back to the Opera House and catch a performance.

CONTENTS

OVERVIEW

"Budapest seems a wonderful place…the impression I had was that we were leaving the West and entering the East. The most western of splendid bridges over the Danube, which is here of noble width and depth, took us among the traditions of Turkish rule." The opening lines of Bram Stoker's *Dracula* (1897) convey protagonist Jonathan Harker's sense of entering unknown territory when he reached Budapest on his journey to Transylvania.

Much has changed since Stoker's day, and Hungary is now very much an integral part of Europe. Its capital, Budapest, is a busy, cosmopolitan city with a mushrooming tourist trade. New routes by budget airlines have made Budapest more accessible than ever, yet, for the moment at least, it still manages to retain much of its historic charm.

GEOGRAPHY

Budapest is a city of two distinct parts, divided by the Danube, which, despite the waltz written in its honour, is murky and definitely not blue. The river separates the medieval streets and Roman remains of Buda and Óbuda (meaning Old Buda) from the late nineteenth-century boulevards of Pest.

On the west bank, in Buda, the hills rise majestically above the river. Over a period of 800 years, Castle Hill suffered 31 sieges and was reduced to rubble on numerous occasions, yet

Founding principle

In AD 1036, the wise King Stephen wrote to his son, Emeric: "Make the strangers welcome in this land, let them keep their languages and customs, for weak and fragile is the realm which is based on a single language and culture."

Postcard-perfect Pest

enough has survived for it to remain one of Europe's most appealing medieval enclaves. On the flat ground of the opposite bank lies Pest, a busy city with broad, leafy boulevards lined by handsome Baroque, Neoclassical and Art Nouveau buildings.

Only in 1873 were these two halves united to form the city we know today as Budapest.

CONTEMPORARY BUDAPEST AND ITS PEOPLE

There's a lot more to the city than the historic sites and thermal baths for which it is famous. Budapest's magnificent bridges and its grand riverside views invite comparisons with Paris, Prague and Vienna – as do many features of its cultural life, from coffeehouses and a love of music to its restaurants and wine-producing tradition. The city is also renowned for its friendliness; if a Hungarian sees you looking at a map and scratching your head, it's not uncommon for them to volunteer help.

EMINENT HUNGARIANS

Hungary has churned out many great musicians, the most famous of whom is perhaps Franz Liszt (1811–86), who became president of the Budapest Academy of Music. Writers include poet Sándor Petőfi (1823–49), who became a hero of the European revolutions of 1848, and Arthur Koestler (1905–83). George Soros, business-man and philanthropist, was born in Budapest, as was conductor Sir Georg Solti, who is buried here. Thirteen Nobel Prizes have been won by Hungarians: holography was developed by prize-winning physicist Dennis Gabor, and the Zsigmondy crater on the moon is named after Nobel laureate Richard Zsigmondy, who scooped the award for chemistry in 1925.

Hollywood in its heyday was full of Hungarian talent, including a number of big-hitting producers and directors – Korda, Fox, Zukor and the much-revered Michael Curtiz who directed *Casablanca*. Actors include Béla Lugosi, best known for his role in the 1931 film *Dracula*. More recently, filmmaker György Pálfi has achieved inter-national renown for *Hukkle* (2002), director László Nemes received

A LASTING IMPRESSION

"Good men must die, but death cannot kill their names," says an old proverb. In Budapest, many of the streets are named after Hungarian heroes. Some are historical figures, others belong to the more recent past. The writer and humourist George Mikes (who wrote *How to be an Alien*, a celebrated satirical book about England) returned to Budapest and found that his former friends had become "streets, statues and boulevards…with a largish square, you once had a drunken fight at 3am in City Park. And that statue there – so majestic on his pedestal – used to go to bed with one of your girlfriends. It hurt very much at the time – it was certainly not the behaviour you expect from a statue."

an Oscar for *Son of Saul* (2015), and director Steven Bognar won an Oscar for his documentary *American Factory* in 2020.

Hungaria's contribution to the modern world is considerable. What would we do without the ball-point pen invented by László Biro? And the frustrating cube designed by Ernő Rubik in the mid-1970s, and tackled by many a teenager, was a huge success.

Trams trundle through the city, whatever the weather

CITY ATTRACTIONS

Budapest has a lot to offer. First and foremost, it's a spa city, so you can experience bathing, health and beauty treatments as well as holistic therapies in wonderfully decadent surroundings. It is also a city of culture; the banks of the Danube, the Castle district of Buda, and Andrássy út and the surrounding historical area are all UNESCO World Heritage Sites. Hungarian cuisine has made great advances lately and a new generation of chefs in Budapest are producing innovative dishes, often based on traditional Magyar recipes.

Getting around Budapest is easy, either on foot or by the highly efficient public transport system (see page 128).

Areas of natural beauty such as the Buda Hills are easily accessible from the city centre, as are the towns and villages strung along the scenic Danube Bend. However, if you have a limited time to spend here, you may well find so much to divert you in the city itself that these excursions have to be saved for another occasion.

HISTORY AND CULTURE

The Carpathian and Danube basins have been inhabited since around 350,000 BC, according to archeological evidence – fragments of bone and pottery – some of which can be seen in collections on display at the Hungarian National Museum in Budapest. However, the first identified occupants were a Celtic-Illyrian tribe, the Eraviscans, refugees from wars in Greece, who settled in the area of today's Budapest in the 3rd century BC. They established a tribal capital on top of Gellért Hill and a settlement in Óbuda.

Some people believe they called the Óbuda settlement Ak Ink (meaning Ample Water), which accounts for the later Roman name, Aquincum. Others believe the Roman name comes from *aqua*, the Latin for water and *quinque* meaning five. Either option points to the importance of water when the settlement was founded.

ENTER THE ROMANS

In the 1st century AD, Roman legions advanced to the Danube. By the 2nd century, 20,000 Roman troops had been deployed along the river between Vienna and Budapest. The Romans built a military camp called Aquincum to command and coordinate this long frontier. The camp became home to 6000 soldiers, and civilian suburbs housing up to 10 times that number of people grew from it. In AD 106 Aquincum was made the capital of the Roman province of Lower Pannonia.

As the Roman Empire crumbled, the forces of Attila the Hun besieged and captured the settlement and established a town on the west side of the river, which they named after Attila's brother, Buda. When Attila died in AD 453, the Avars overthrew the Huns and occupied the area until the 9th century.

MAGYAR MIGRATION

The Magyars date their arrival to AD 890. Their origins are a mystery, though they are thought to have come from the area between the Volga River and the Urals. The name Magyar stuck for both the country (Hungary is called *Magyarország* in Hungarian) and the language (*magyar*). Related tribes are thought to have travelled north-west to modern Finland and Estonia. Their distantly related tongues are classified by linguists as Finno-Ugric.

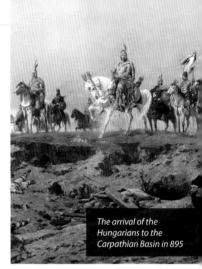

The arrival of the Hungarians to the Carpathian Basin in 895

The first military leader of the Magyars, Prince Árpád, founded a dynasty that lasted more than three centuries. Prince Géza, his great-grandson, embraced Christianity, and on Christmas Day 1000, Géza's son, István (Stephen) was crowned first king of Hungary in Esztergom. Stephen built churches and spread Christianity and was canonized as Szent István (St Stephen). A landmark document of this medieval civilization was the Golden Bull of 1222, a charter that clarified the rights of nobles and commoners. In 1241–2, however, the country was invaded by the Mongols.

Whole towns and villages, including Buda and Pest, were devastated by an orgy of killing and destruction, followed by famine and epidemics. The Mongols retreated, however, and King Béla IV set about restoring the nation, wisely constructing the rebuilt town of Buda within strong, fortified walls.

Early government

The Golden Bull was promulgated by King András II after his nobles grew tired of his profligate ways. It created the framework for the Diet, an annual meeting of noblemen.

TRADE AND CULTURE

The Árpád dynasty ended in 1301 and Károly Róbert (Charles Robert) claimed the crown. Although he was an Angevin (a member of the ruling family of Anjou in France), his paternal grandmother was the daughter of Stephen V and she aroused Károly's interest in Hungary when he was a boy. He had to fight for control and underwent three coronations by various factions, the final one with the traditional holy crown. A man of great ability, Károly ruled well. Originally, he set up his court in Visegrád but soon decided to move it to Budapest. He was thwarted for five years but eventually gained access by subterfuge and executed recalcitrant officials. A palace was built and trade was stimulated; Buda became the capital and Pest a commercial centre with city walls. Today's Kiskörút, or 'Little Boulevard', follows the line of the old walls.

Other kings followed but the next major figure was János Hunyadi, a Transylvanian and national hero of the mid-fifteenth century. The Ottoman Turks had been threatening the country for some time, and Hunyadi led the resistance. When the young Polish king, chosen to rule Hungary after the death of Albrecht of Habsburg, was slain in the battle of Varna in 1444, Hunyadi became regent. When Albrecht's son, Ladislaus V, came of age, Hunyadi resumed his fight. He led the Hungarian army to victory against the Ottomans at Nándorfehérvár (now Belgrade) in 1456. When Ladislaus V died without an heir in 1458, János Hunyadi's son, Korvin Mátyás (Matthias Corvinus Hunyadi), was elected to the throne. For the next 32 years, Hungary enjoyed a golden age of intellectual and civic development. Under the enlightened rule of Matthias, the city of Buda and the new palace became the focus of the country's cultural rebirth, and Pest flourished as the hub of trade and industry.

In 1490, Mátyás also died without an heir. The Hungarian barons extended their power, and a council of 39 took control, but failed to deal with the growing threat of the Ottoman Turks. In 1514, the barons armed 40,000 peasants, who were led by an officer called György Dósza. However, when assembled at Pest, the peasants showed that they had ideas of their own, and rebelled against the barons. Their resistance was unsuccessful and they were reduced to serfdom; Dósza was executed. The Turkish forces were now superior and there was no effective opposition. The king, Lajos (Louis) II, and much of his army, were killed at the battle of Mohács

The magnificent Royal Palace still dominates the Buda skyline

in southern Hungary in 1526, and Hungary disappeared from the map of Europe for the next four centuries.

The Habsburg rulers of neighbouring Austria, fearful that Vienna would be the Ottoman Empire's next conquest, proclaimed themselves rulers of Hungary in order to create a buffer zone between themselves and the Turks. Hungary was dismembered, with a narrow strip going to the Habsburgs, Transylvania becoming a principality under the Sultan's authority, and central Hungary fell under direct Turkish rule. Turkish occupation lasted a century and a half, although it left behind little of note except the thermal baths.

THE HABSBURGS

In 1686–7, the Holy Alliance (comprising the Habsburgs, Poland and Venice) liberated Buda. Many Hungarians, however, wanted independence, not Habsburg rule. From 1703–11, Prince Ferenc Rákóczi (a descendant of the princes of Transylvania) became leader of the struggle for independence. A peasant uprising soon turned into a battle for liberation, but the country was too ravaged by war and poverty to sustain a rebellion.

Peace lasted for the rest of the eighteenth century, during which the country made great economic strides as a province of the Habsburg Empire. Pest expanded its role in international trade while Buda regained its status as Hungary's administrative hub. There was a period of reform during which Hungarians such

MEMORIALS TO THE PAST

In Budapest, you can stroll through history. The Kerepesi Cemetery was the original national place of burial, and many who shaped the nation's events are buried there – including Ferenc Deák, Lajos Kossuth and the journalists, writers and bohemians who were the original habitués of the coffeehouses. Nearby lie the ranks of middle-class families: the Gerbeauds, respected restaurateurs, for example; and several chess grand masters – the days long gone since they opened with the Budapest gambit.

The communist regime discouraged religious burials, so in allowing such funerals, Farkasreti Cemetery came to the fore. The graves of Bartók, Kodály and Sir Georg Solti can be found here. Imre Makovecz designed the mortuary chapel; the interior is a simulacrum of the human body, in which the dead lie at the heart. The mausoleums and other works of art that mark the graves range from the beautiful to the kitsch.

Hungarian cemeteries are also the place to find wooden gravemarkers, beautifully worked but with no inscriptions, as the carved icons carry all the important information about the deceased.

Remember, though, that thousands have no memorials: the revolutionaries of 1956, for example, were buried where they fell.

as Count István Széchenyi secured development and economic reforms, while Lajos Kossuth sought social changes. In 1847, these two men, with Ferenc Deák and Count Lajos Batthyány, formed a liberal opposition party.

In 1848, a group of young intellectuals, including the 25-year-old radical poet, Sándor Petőfi, led a rebellion. They formed a short-lived provisional government, headed by Kossuth. The Emperor Franz Josef I summoned help from the Tsar of Russia, and crushed the revolt the following year.

Something had to be done, and the solution was proposed by Deák. The Compromise of 1867 turned the Austrian Empire into the Austro-Hungarian Empire, and made Franz Josef dual monarch. His wife Elizabeth (Erzsébet), popularly known as Sisi, was known to have been helpful and sympathetic to the Hungarian cause. Franz Josef and Elizabeth were crowned as rulers, and Count Gulya Andrássy (who may have been one of Elizabeth's lovers) became prime minister.

RAPID GROWTH

In the period between the Compromise and World War I, Budapest grew faster than any other city in Europe. Industry, banking and commerce ensured economic growth, and grand buildings sprang up across the city. Count Széchenyi, who was a powerful force in the development of the city, is credited with responsibility for the Chain Bridge, which was the first such structure to span the Danube. It is said that he was motivated by frustration

National hero

In the 1840s, Lajos Kossuth (1802–94) became a popular hero across Europe. He was a fervent nationalist, and under his influence, Hungarian finally replaced Latin as the language for laws, education and government business.

at having to wait a week to get across the river by boat to bury his father. It was Széchenyi who had the idea of uniting the towns of Buda, Óbuda and Pest into one city, and in 1873 Budapest was born.

In 1896, the nation celebrated the 1000th anniversary of the settlement of the Pannonian plains by the Magyars. Hősök tere (Heroes' Square), the Országház (Houses of Parliament), Vajdahunyad Castle, the

Hungary's coat-of-arms

metro system under Andrássy út, the Opera House and other important developments date from this heady time. The city's wealth triggered the blossoming of fashionable confectioners, shops and entertainment venues. Tourists arrived to 'take the cure' in the waters of Budapest's spas. Along with the cure, they also took coffee and pastries, just as visitors do today, at *Ruszwurm*, *Gerbeaud*, *Lukács*, *Café Művész*, the *Centrál Kávéház* and the *New York Kávéház*.

THE EARLY TWENTIETH CENTURY

While Budapest may have been Europe's fastest-growing city in 1900, within a mere two decades it had been pushed back to its former status as a nondescript town of peripheral importance. World War I brought the good times to an end. Austro-Hungary was defeated, and the empire collapsed. An independent republic was set up under Count Mihály Károlyi. He resigned in March 1919 and a Communist Party, led by Béla Kun, established a Soviet Republic.

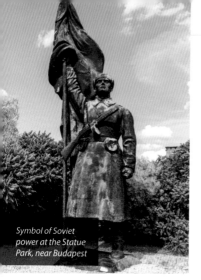

Symbol of Soviet power at the Statue Park, near Budapest

However, this was brought down shortly afterwards, in July, when the country was occupied and looted by Romanian forces.

In 1920, Admiral Miklós Horthy was proclaimed regent. Although the country was a monarchy once again, it was decided not to recall the king. It was an unusual situation – a powerful admiral in a landlocked country, appointed regent of a monarchy without a king.

WORLD WAR II

An uneasy alliance with Germany existed throughout World War II, ending in March 1944 when German troops occupied Hungary. However, the Soviet Army was advancing fast. The Germans were defeated after a 14-week siege, and Budapest fell in February 1945. By the time the Russians assumed control of the city, three-quarters of its buildings had been destroyed and the Hungarian death toll had reached half a million.

SOVIET RULE

In 1949, Hungary was transformed into a People's Republic under Soviet rule. Forced public displays of loyalty could not disguise the fact that living standards were low and dissatisfaction was high. Stalinist leader Mátyás Rákosi established the sinister avo secret police to ensure compliance with party doctrine by rooting out 'class enemies'.

After eight years of brutal repression, 50,000 students and workers marched on parliament to air their grievances on 23 October 1956. Angry students toppled a giant statue of Stalin near Heroes' Square, and the police fired on protesters outside the Hungarian Radio headquarters. The protest snowballed into a potent popular uprising that drew worldwide attention. Within days, a provisional Hungarian Government, led by the reformer Imre Nagy, had withdrawn Hungary from the Warsaw Pact. Soviet retribution took just 12 days. On 4 November, Red Army tanks rolled into Budapest and quickly crushed the resistance. The West watched in horror as Nagy and thousands more were executed. Some 25,000 Hungarians died and 200,000 fled the country.

The Soviets installed János Kádár as the new party boss. Although his rule began with repression, Kádár introduced some reforms, and in 1968, the New Economic Mechanism allowed a limited form of consumerism, known as 'goulash socialism'. In 1988–9, with the effects of *glasnost* and *perestroika* being felt throughout the Eastern bloc, Hungary experienced many changes. Restrictions on foreign travel were lifted, and demonstrations prompted the Central Committee of the Communist Party to allow free elections in a multi-party system. The People's Republic was terminated, and the Republic of Hungary was proclaimed.

Hungary tore a gaping hole in the Iron Curtain by dismantling the barbed-wire barrier along the Austrian border. In 1990, the country held its first

The 1956 uprising

The revolution of 1956 came about because Hungarians took all too literally Soviet leader Khrushchev's new doctrine of 'different roads to socialism'. The ferocity with which the Soviets destroyed the revolution – and the Hungarian Government – showed that no such roads were open.

free elections in 43 years and again became a democratic republic. In 1991, the last Soviet soldier left, and in 1999 Hungary joined Nato.

INTO THE EU

On 1 May 2004, there were fireworks, celebrations and flag-waving as Hungary became a fully-fledged member of the EU, following a vote the previous year. The then Prime Minister Péter Medgyessy said, 'We can't expect Europe to offer a miracle. The miracle isn't within Europe. The miracle is within us.' Certainly, the following years proved challenging. Ineffective budgetary management made the country vulnerable to the world financial crisis of 2008, and to avoid the collapse of its currency, Hungary negotiated a $20 billion bail-out with the IMF. The people signalled their frustration in the 2010 elections, replacing Socialists with Conservatives, and Fidesz leader Viktor Orbán took the office of Prime Minister. In 2014 parliamentary elections, the ruling party won a sweeping victory, staying in power.

During the migrant crisis in 2015, Hungary built a fence on its borders with Serbia and Croatia and in the 2016 referendum, the majority of Hungarians pronounced themselves against the EU's migrant quota. In 2017, János Áder of Fidesz won a second term as the president of Hungary; he was succeeded in 2022 by Katalin Novák, Hungary's first female president.

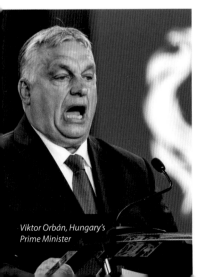
Viktor Orbán, Hungary's Prime Minister

IMPORTANT DATES

1st century AD Roman legions advance to the Danube.

890 The Magyars arrive in the area.

1000 Coronation of King (later St) Stephen.

1222 Proclamation of the Golden Bull, Hungary's Magna Carta.

1241–2 Mongol invasion destroys villages; famine and epidemics rife.

1301 Foundation of the Angevin dynasty by Károly Róbert.

1456 Hunyadi's victory over the Ottomans at battle of Nándorfehérvár.

1458–90 Rule of Mátyás Corvinus Hunyadi.

1526 Battle of Móhacs divides Hungary and ushers in Ottoman rule.

1686–7 Liberation of Budapest by the Holy Alliance.

1703–11 Unsuccessful independence struggle, led by Ferenc Rákóczi.

1848–9 Rebellion of intellectuals, led by Sándor Petőfi.

1867 Foundation of the Austro-Hungarian Empire.

1873 Budapest formed from Buda, Pest and Óbuda.

1896 Celebration of 1,000 years since the Magyars settled in Hungary.

1944 Hungary falls to German forces.

1945 Soviet Army defeats Germans; repressive Soviet rule ensues.

1956 The Hungarian revolution is brutally crushed by the Soviet Union.

1958 Imre Nagy, prime minister during the 1956 revolt, is executed.

1988–9 The Communist Party responds to public dissatisfaction as Soviet leader Gorbachev promises no more interference in Hungarian affairs.

1989 Republic of Hungary proclaimed.

1990 Free elections return the Conservative Democratic Forum.

2004 Hungary joins the EU.

2006 Riots follow Prime Minister Gyurcsany's admission of lying.

2008 Financial crisis forces Hungary to agree 220 billion loan with IMF.

2010 Economic woes bring electoral disaster for the Socialist Party.

2014 Ruling party Fidesz, led by Viktor Orbán, wins parliamentary elections.

2016 The majority reject the EU's migrant quota in the referendum.

2020 On 4 March, the first cases of COVID-19 are announced in Hungary; by 18 May, the virus had spread to every part of the country.

2022 In March, Katalin Novák is elected as the first female President of Hungary.

Hungary's mighty Parliament

OUT AND ABOUT

Getting around Budapest is relatively easy, as the majority of sights are clustered in the central areas. Castle Hill is well set up for walking, as are many of the wide city boulevards such as Andrássy út and the pedestrianized Váci utca. Much of the town is served by the metro or by buses, trolley-buses, trams and the HÉV suburban railways.

For the most part, this section of the Guide follows the natural layout of the city, starting on the western bank with Buda, Óbuda (Old Buda, just north of Buda) and the Buda Hills (further north-west), before crossing the Danube to Pest on the eastern bank. Then there is Margaret Island, a sliver of land cast adrift in the Danube, excursions in the city suburbs and trips further afield.

BUDA'S CASTLE HILL AND OLD TOWN

The best place to begin a city tour is **Castle Hill** ❶ (Varhegy – *hegy* means hill), a steep limestone outcrop that rises 50–60m metres (165–200ft) above the Danube. Castle Hill overlooks Pest from a long, narrow plateau divided into two sections. The southern part is occupied by the enormous Baroque palace of Buda Castle, situated on the grounds where the original castle from 1265 once stood, while the north-ern district consists of the Vár, or Old Town. This corner of Budapest has seen waves of destruction from invaders over the years, from Turks and Habsburgs to the Nazis and

Impotent pigeons

You might notice that pigeons are somewhat less common in Budapest public squares than in other cities; it is rumoured that the city authorities have contraceptive pills ground up in the bird food.

the Soviets, and many of its sites have been rebuilt more than once. Nowadays, however, the only invaders are of a peaceful nature: curious tourists coming to admire the picturesque, historic streets – protected as a World Heritage Site since 1988.

There are various ways of reaching Castle Hill. The most popular method is aboard the nineteenth-century funicular (*sikló*; daily 7.30am–10pm), which begins just beyond the end of the Chain Bridge and rises to Buda Castle. As you approach the *sikló* terminus, notice the strange, oval-shaped structure beside the path. This is not a modern art installation, but the **kilometre stone**, from which all distances in Hungary are measured.

Alternatives to the funicular include the bus service (Várbusz) that trundles up Castle Hill on its way between Széll Kálmán tér (Moszkva tér from 1951 to 2011) to the west and Deák Ferenc tér on the other side of the river in central Pest. You can also climb the hill on foot, but cars are generally not allowed unless you are staying at the *Hilton*.

BUDA CASTLE

Buda Castle ❷ (Budai Vár), referred to in the past as the Royal Palace, lies to the left as you emerge from the funicular and

TURUL BIRDS

Turul birds are mythical eagles, sometimes shown carrying the flaming sword of God, and are a powerful symbol in Hungary. The bird is said to have sired both Attila the Hun and Almos, father of Árpád, who led the Magyar conquest of the Carpathian Basin in the ninth century. The link with Attila gave Árpád the right to reconquer his lands. The best-known example of a turul is probably the one at Szent György tér, next to the upper terminal of the Budavári Sikló (funicular). You can spot four more on top of the Liberty Bridge.

Buda Castle

dominates Castle Hill's southern skyline. Begun in the thirteenth century, the palace reached its zenith in the 1400s under King Mátyás, when it was considered the equal of any Renaissance palace in Europe. By the sixteenth century, sturdy ramparts had been erected for defence. The Turks took Buda by trickery, not by siege, but under the Ottoman Empire the palace fell into disrepair. The siege of 1686 saw it recaptured and placed under Habsburg rule, but the castle was almost wholly demolished, and the area became a backwater.

In the eighteenth century, the Baroque town developed, and after the War of Hungarian Independence in 1849, the new government established its administrative centre in the castle district. After World War I, the country's regent, Miklós Horthy, had the run of the palace. When his reign came to an end during the next war, the German forces took over, and made the palace their headquarters during their final stand in 1945. It therefore became the target

Hungarian National Gallery in Buda Castle

for devastating Soviet shelling from across the river. During the communist era that followed, the palace was rebuilt – mostly in the 1950s and 1960s – to house some of Hungary's most important museums.

If you are climbing Castle Hill, the best approach to the palace is from the steps at the southern tip of the hill beside the Semmelweis Museum (see page 42). The stone path wends through gardens to the rear entrance of the castle and the only surviving turreted tower, the **Buzogány (Mace) Tower**. Steps lead up through the castle gardens to the entrance of the **Budapest History Museum** (Budapesti Történeti Múzeum; www.btm.hu; Tues–Sun 10am–6pm) in Wing E of Buda Castle. The museum charts the development of the city from the fifth century onwards.

HUNGARIAN NATIONAL GALLERY

The palace and its collections are vast, and too extensive to see in a single day. Wings B, C and D house the **Hungarian National Gallery ❸** (Magyar Nemzeti Galéria; www.mng.hu; Tues–Sun 10am–6pm, last entry 5pm), which has a fine collection of medieval and Gothic art as well as displays of Hungarian Impressionism and twentieth-century works (Wings C and D). Several rooms on the first floor are dedicated to Mihály Munkácsy, a nineteenth-century painter who became famous in Paris. His pictures are dark and gloomy in theme as well as literally, and became even more so as a result of the bitumen he mixed with his paint. Look out also for the works of Hungarian painters József Rippl-Rónai and Károly Lotz, as well as János Vaszary's pivotal *Golden Age* and the odd but striking works of Tivadar Kosztka Csontváry.

The southern courtyard includes Wing F, which houses the two million volumes of the **Széchenyi National Library** (Széchenyi könyvtár Bibliothek; www.oszk.hu).

MÁTYÁS CHURCH

The **Old Town** essentially consists of four parallel streets, packed with colourful houses, historic monuments and small museums. A short walk to the right of the funicular terminus brings you to Dísz tér (Parade Square), which separates the northern section of the district from the palace area.

THE LUDWIG COLLECTION

Anybody interested in contemporary art should head for the Ludwig Collection – Museum of Contemporary Art (Kortárs Művészeti Múzeum; www.ludwigmuseum.hu; permanent exhibition Tues–Sun 10am–6pm, temporary exhibitions until 8pm) in the Palace of Arts (Művészetek Palotája) on the east bank of the Danube to the south of the Belváros near the Lágymányosi Bridge, in Komor Marcell utca 1. Established in 1991 by Peter and Irene Ludwig, a German couple with collections in Aachen, Cologne and Vienna, it includes works by leading members of the American Pop Art movement – Andy Warhol, Roy Lichtenstein, Robert Rauschenberg and Claes Oldenburg. The Ludwigs also amassed a huge curation of works by Picasso; several are exhibited here.

The 80-metre (260ft) spire of the **Mátyás (Matthias) Church ❹** (Mátyás templom; www.matyas-templom.hu; Mon–Fri 9am–5pm (Thurs until 4.30pm), Sat 9am–2pm, Sun 1–5pm) towers gracefully over the historic district. The crow that can be seen above the church refers to King Mátyás Corvinus Hunyadi (1458–90), whose nickname 'Corvinus' came from the symbol on his coat-of-arms (*corvinus* means crow), which can be seen on the tower. He was Hungary's most popular medieval king and was married here (twice) in the fifteenth century. The Habsburg Emperor Franz Josef I was also crowned King of Hungary here, in 1867, to the tune of the *Coronation Mass*, composed for the occasion by Franz Liszt (1811–86).

The original church was built in the mid-thirteenth century, converted into a mosque during the Turkish occupation, and seriously damaged during the reconquest of Buda in 1686. It was rebuilt in Baroque style after the return of the Christian forces, and between 1873 and 1896, it was completely reconstructed along its present neo-Gothic lines. The unusual diamond-patterned roof, the geometric designs on the interior walls and the stained-glass windows and frescoes date from refurbishment in the nineteenth century.

In the **Loreto Chapel**, immediately to the left of the entrance, stands a treasured red-marble statue of the Virgin. A staircase, entered on the left-hand side of the church, leads to the entrance to the crypt and to the **Collection of Ecclesiastical Art**. The museum rambles up and down various old staircases, offering an excellent view, at one point, down onto the nave. There is a fine collection of medieval stone carvings, historic vestments, religious paintings, and relics, including a replica of the **Crown of St Stephen**.

In Trinity Square (Szentháromság tér) in front of the church is the **Holy Trinity Column**, crowded with statues of saints and angels. It was erected in 1713 by grateful survivors of a plague epidemic. Across the square, towards Dísz tér, the white, two-storey Baroque building with a jutting corner balcony served as Buda's town hall from 1710 to 1873. Along the adjacent **Szentháromság utca** (the street that joins the four parallel streets alongside Mátyás Church), notice the medieval barrel-vaulted doorways on your way to No. 7, the **Ruszwurm** confectionery shop (www.ruszwurm.hu).

One of the most prestigious in Europe, it was founded in 1827 and is still going strong. Nothing has changed since its early days: the cosy Biedermeyer-style furnishings have survived all the vicissitudes of the past two centuries, and the cakes and pastries are still irresistible.

FISHERMAN'S BASTION

Immediately behind Mátyás Church is the intriguingly named **Fisherman's Bastion ⑤** (Halászbástya), built onto the castle walls.

At first glance, this romantic array of turrets, terraces and arches resembles a fairy-tale castle and could pass for a medieval fortification. In fact, it was constructed around the turn of the twentieth century purely for ornamental reasons (and therefore perfectly fulfilling its brief). The monument's name is probably a reference to the fishermen who defended the ramparts here in the eighteenth century. If you want to walk around the upper turrets and towers, you will have to pay a small

The romantic Fisherman's Bastion

entry fee; the views across the Danube to Parliament from down below are much the same, but free. Nearby is the equestrian statue of King Stephen (István), the first king of Hungary, who was canonized in 1083. Elderly women trade Transylvanian tablecloths here, and street musicians fill the air with the sounds of Bartók and Liszt.

Just west of the Fisherman's Bastion is the somewhat jarring facade of the six-storey *Budapest Hilton Hotel*. The bold approach of merging ancient and modern has integrated this 1977 hotel with the remains of a seventeenth-century Jesuit college and the tower of a thirteenth-century Dominican monastery, the result of which is not to everyone's taste. Across Hess András tér, the bas-relief on the **Red Hedgehog** at No. 3 is the sign from the building's days as an inn during the eighteenth century. No. 4 is the place where the first book in Hungarian was printed in 1473, by András Hess.

TOURING THE OLD TOWN

Begin your tour of the district's old streets along delightful Táncsics Mihály utca. At No. 7, where Beethoven stayed in 1800, is the **Museum of Music History** (www.budacastlebudapest. com/museum-music-history; Tues–Sun 10am–4pm), where you will find orchestral instruments from Haydn's day, Hungarian folk instruments and the archive of Béla Bartók. Next door, at No. 9, are plaques paying homage to the political heroes **Mihály Táncsics** and **Lajos Kossuth**, both imprisoned here in the 1830s and 1840s for their nationalist beliefs. No. 26 served as a synagogue from the late fourteenth century and has a small museum. The street ends at the **Vienna Gate** (Bécsi kapu), a reminder that the district was once fully enclosed. The grand structure to the left of the gate, with the diamond-patterned roof, echoing that of Mátyás Church, houses the **National Archives**. Doubling back on **Fortuna utca**, you walk down an attractive street of pastel-painted houses. It takes its name from a tavern that stood at No. 4, from 1785 to 1868.

A colourful façade in Fortuna utca, in the Old Town

Returning to Szentháromság tér, head north again, this time on **Országház utca**. *Országház* means Houses of Parliament, and the street takes its name from the parliamentary sessions that took place in the building at No. 28 between 1790 and 1807. The architectural highlights here include the grand fifteenth-century mansion, now occupied by the **Alabárdos** restaurant (Halbadier; www.alabardos.hu; currently closed for restoration works), and Nos 18–22, which are considered among the finest examples of four-teenth- and fifteenth-century domestic architecture on the hill. Several other buildings incorporate picturesque medieval features, at times hidden just inside the arches. Here, you will see ancient stone *sedilia* (built-in seats for three people) and strings of paprika hung out to dry across windows and balconies.

At the end of Országház utca rises the ruined **Church of Mary Magdalene ❻**, converted to a mosque under the Turks and reduced to knee-high remains by the Allies in the last days of

World War II. Amazingly, its huge fifteenth-century tower survived. One stone-traceried window was rebuilt, but the rest of the church was left in ruins as a poignant reminder of wartime destruction. A more light-hearted curiosity is visible on the corner of Országház utca and Nándor utca, but you have to look up to see it. A 'flying nun' (a convent occupied No. 28 before the parliament) has apparently passed straight through the corner of the building. Miklós Melocco executed this whimsical sculpture in 1977.

Úri utca (Gentlemen's Street) is even more ancient than Országház utca, and the houses have some fascinating details. There's another specialist museum at No. 49: the **Postal Museum** (Telefonia Múzeum; www.postamuzeum.hu; Tues–Sun summer 10am–6pm, winter until 4pm) proudly claims that in 1881, Budapest had the world's first telephone exchange.

Buda Castle Labyrinth

No. 9 Úri utca was the entrance to the **Buda Castle Labyrinth** (Budavári Labirintus; www.budacastlebudapest.com/labyrinth-under-the-castle-hill Tues–Sun 10am–7pm, last entry 6.30pm), a maze of tunnels, some of which were created by natural hydro-thermal activity and other that were man-made as cellars and bomb shelters. The tunnels themselves are filled with artefacts and historical information, though you may need to make use of the torch on your phone to see much of it. It's dark and creepy in this subterranean network, as well as being a little chilly; an extra layer is a good idea.

Úri utca terminates at Dísz tér, where it is best to turn and walk back along Tárnok utca. The **Arany Hordó** (Golden Barrel; www.aranyhordovendeglo.hu) restaurant stands out, with orange-and-red geometric frescoes painted on the overhanging first floor. Next door, No. 18 was built as a merchant's house in the first half of the fifteenth century. From 1740 until 1913, it was the **Golden Eagle Pharmacy** (Arany Sas Patikaház), but today it is the most attractive and idiosyncratic of the district's small museums, the Pharmacy Museum (www.semmelweismuseum.hu/arany-sas-patikamuzeum; Tues–Sun 10am–6pm). Beautiful old majolica vessels sit alongside informative displays on the potions and alchemical practices deployed in Budapest. Look out in particular for the 2000-year-old mummified head that was used to provide the 'mummy-head dust' prescribed for treating bronchitis.

The last street in this district is leafy Tóth Árpád sétány. This promenade, which runs along the western ramparts, offers views of the Buda Hills, the huge southern railway station (Déli pályaudvar) and **Vérmező Park**. The name of this green space translates as 'the field of blood' and pays homage to the victims of a massacre here in 1795: Hungarian Jacobins who were considered dangerous as they disseminated the ideas of the Enlightenment and opposed the monarchy. Tóth Árpád sétany is the perfect place for a stroll, particularly in the early evening, when Budapestis come out to enjoy the fresh air. At the northern end, assorted cannons guard the entrance to the **Museum of Military History** ➐ (Hadtörténeti Múzeum; www.militaria.hu; Tues–Sun 10am–5pm). The extensive armaments exhibition is popular with children, while the section dedicated to the 1956 uprising (see page 23) is likely to make the most impact on older visitors.

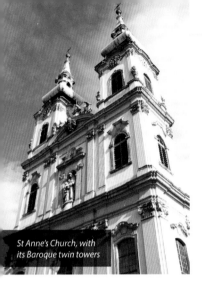

St Anne's Church, with its Baroque twin towers

BUDA RIVERSIDE

VIZIVÁROS (WATERTOWN)

The district between Castle Hill and the Danube is called **Víziváros**, or **Watertown**. In the Middle Ages, the red-roofed district was where commoners lived, beyond the walled area for royalty and wealthier merchants on Castle Hill. During the Ottoman era, the Turks transformed the area's churches into mosques and constructed splendid public baths. Today, the busy urban area is the site of new hotels, built here to capitalize on the proximity to Castle Hill and the unbeatable views of the sprawling Houses of Parliament across the river.

The stretch of riverside to the north of the Chain Bridge shelters a string of attractive arcades and terraces, adorned with Neoclassical statues and ceremonial staircases, as well as gateways (closed to the public) leading up to Buda Castle. The area can be reached on foot from Castle Hill, or by taking the metro, bus, tram, or suburban railway to **Batthyány tér**, a major square and a city transport hub.

The Vienna stagecoach terminal was once just around the corner from Batthyány tér, and the famous **White Cross Inn** (Fehér Kereszt fogadó), a majestic building on the side of the square opposite the river, was a fashionable venue for grand balls and other celebrations. The Venetian libertine, Casanova, is reputed to have stayed here. On the south side of the square rise the twin towers of the fine, Baroque **St Anne's Church** (Szent Anna temp-lom; 1740–62), where in the summer, regular recitals are given on what is reputedly the country's finest church organ.

Further north along **Fő utca** are the **Király Baths ❽** (Király fürdő; www.kiralyfurdo.hu). The name Király, which means king, was the family name of the early nineteenth-century owners of the baths. Originally established by the Turkish Pasha of Budapest in 1565, the authentic Ottoman section has survived, complete with a large, octagonal pool beneath a dome. Sadly, the baths closed during the Covid-19 pandemic and have yet to reopen.

Turn left off Frankel Leó út (the continuation of Fő utca) at Margit híd (Margaret Bridge) and follow signs up the steps to Mecset utca and the **Tomb of Gül Baba** (Gül Baba türbéje) – another memento of Turkish times. Gül Baba was a whirling dervish, killed during the siege of Buda in 1541. Suleiman the Magnificent ordered the tomb to be built, and the Turkish Government have renovated the site. A statue of the great man stands just outside the shrine. There's a story, probably apocryphal, that Gül Baba brought the rose to Budapest. He is known as Father of the Roses, and the hill on which the mausoleum stands is called Rózsadomb (Hill of the Roses). It is now one of the most sought-after addresses in Budapest.

In contrast to the austerity of the mausoleum, the 1896 neo-Gothic **Calvinist Church** is recognized by its exuberant tile-and-brick exterior. It stands along the river towards the Chain Bridge, just to the south of Batthyány tér.

GELLÉRT HILL

While Castle Hill provides arguably the finest views over the River Danube, another lookout point just to the south of Buda Castle should not be missed. **Gellért Hill ❾** (Gellérthegy), which rises some 140 metres (460ft) almost directly above the Danube on the Buda side, affords a wide panorama of the city.

St Gellért

Gellért was a Venetian missionary, Bishop Gerardus, who was martyred in the eleventh century, reputedly by being put into a spike-studded barrel and thrown into the Danube. The place where this horrendous deed was committed was marked in 1902 by the construction of a statue of Gellért, holding a cross, as if he is still blessing the city of Budapest.

The hill is not particularly well served by public transport, although there is a bus, No. 27, from Móricz Zsigmond Körtér that goes most of the way, to Búsuló Juhász (Citadella). The climb, starting from the *Gellért Hotel*, is fortunately not too strenuous for non-disabled people, and there are seats and views to compensate for your efforts. As you head higher, you may see flowers, birds and, in particular, butterflies – Hungary is reputed to have more butterflies than anywhere else in Europe. To the right as you set out, look out for the extraordinary and atmospheric **Rock Cave Church** (Sziklatemplom; www.sziklatemplom.hu; Mon–Sat 9.30am–7.30pm), which belongs to the Order of St Paul, the only monastic body of Hungarian origin.

The **Citadel** (Citadella) crowning the hill was built by the Austrians after the Revolution of 1848 as a lookout point from which to control adjacent Castle Hill. Despised by Hungarians as a symbol of occupation, the Citadel saw no action, however, until the end of World War II, when German forces were trapped here and kept the city under fire until they surrendered. The Citadel has been renovated but the panoramic views are worth the visit alone.

The 40-metre (132ft) tall **Liberty Statue** (or Szabadság szobor), which is visible from all parts of the city, stands slightly below the citadel. The Russians erected it in memory of their troops who fell fighting the Germans. The monument is loathed by the majority of local people as a symbol of Soviet domination, but it has become too much of a city landmark to remove – although some of its elements have now been relegated to the Statue Park (see page 76).

At the base of the hill, the **Gellért Hotel and Baths** ⑩ (Gellért Szálló és fürdő) is the perfect place to recover from your walk. Behind the classic 1918 Art Nouveau structure is a huge, landscaped outdoor swimming pool complex, while inside (entry on Kelenhegyi út 4) are the finest thermal baths in Buda (www.gellertbath.hu; daily 9am–7pm). The unisex indoor pool has a vaulted glass ceiling and Roman-style carved columns, while the thermal baths (with mixed and unisex sections) are adorned with marble statues, mosaics and glazed tiles.

Although the Gellért reigns supreme among Budapest's thermal baths, there are two more historic baths (fürdő) along the Buda embankment, located near the Erzsébet híd (Elizabeth Bridge). The entrance to the **Rudas Baths** ⑪ (www.rudasfurdo.hu; swimming pool daily 6am–10pm, also night bathing Fri–Sat 10pm–3am; see website for detailed opening times of single-sex baths) is at Döbrentei tér 9. The baths were opened in 1550, and although the building has been much altered over the centuries, the timeless atmosphere is authentic as ever in the steamy main pool, where a stone Turkish dome curves above an octagonal pool, and sunlight streams in through the star-shaped glass openings in the grand cupola.

The stunning view from Gellért Hill

Rudas Baths, opened in 1550

The **Semmelweis Museum** ⑫ (Semmelweis Orvostörténeti Múzeum; Tues–Sun 10am–6pm) on Apród utca 1–3, is named after physician and scientist Ignác Semmelweis. Here, you can learn about old-fashioned medical instruments and techniques, some of which appear worse than the conditions they were intended to relieve. There is also a beautifully preserved pharmacy, dating from 1813.

ÓBUDA

Óbuda – Old Buda – is the most ancient section of the city, being the site of the Roman city of Aquincum, built in the first century AD as the capital of the province of Lower Pannonia. The 'aqua' part of the Roman name suggests the importance of building a settlement close to the water. Nowadays, the area is scarred by heavy traffic using the main northern highway out of the city, and blighted by vast, cheaply constructed, Soviet-era apartment blocks. It is in this unlikely setting that Hungary's most impressive Roman ruins are found.

The civilian town of **Aquincum**, built for artisans, merchants, priests and other non-military staff, can be reached by hév train from Batthyány tér in twenty minutes. Just past the Auchan hypermarket, the remains of a Roman aqueduct can be seen in the central carriageway of the motorway, running close to the railway.

The archeological site covers a large area and comprises the foundations of villas, workshops and public areas. You will need to stoke the imagination to recreate the scene as it was when 40,000 people lived here nearly 2000 years ago, though you can find inspiration in the attached **Aquincum Museum** (Szentendrei út 139; www.aquincum.hu; exhibitions Tues–Sun: April–Oct 10am–6pm; Nov–March 10am–4pm, archeological park April–Oct 9am–6pm, Nov–March 10am–4pm). Here, the best of the finds are displayed, including tombstones, statues, mosaics and the remains of a water-powered organ (since reconstructed so it can be played).

Returning towards Batthyány tér, more Roman ruins are located near Arpád hid (and near the bus terminal at Szentélek tér, if you want to catch a bus back). If you enter the subway beneath the Flórián tér overpass, you'll find assorted Roman remains and a

PROFESSOR SEMMELWEIS

Ignác Semmelweis was born in Buda in 1815. While working in a hospital in Vienna, he noticed that cases of puerperal fever ran at 13 percent among patients treated by doctors and at only two percent among women treated by midwives. The death of a friend who had cut his finger while performing an autopsy and who died of symptoms similar to puerperal fever alerted Semmelweis to the fact that doctors did autopsies first thing in the morning, before going on to examine living patients. He had the idea that doctors should wash their hands between examinations. This notion was not well received at first, but the hand-washing achieved sweeping reductions to rates of infection. Despite this, Semmelweis suffered from the attitude of colleagues who thought him a charlatan. Eventually, he was admitted to a mental health institution and, it is said, died when a cut on his hand became infected.

Aquincum Museum

singular sight – Roman baths, open to the sky, beneath the central reservation of the motorway. Take the subway exit on the opposite side from the baths to see another incongruous sight: a dozen isolated Corinthian columns set against the backdrop of a 1960s housing estate. The columns are on a grassy piece of parkland where local people walk their dogs. There are various other ruins to be seen here, and it's a good place to picnic.

The remains of the amphitheatre of the military town are further south on the corner of Pacsirtamező utca and Nagyszombat utca. Gladiators performed here in the second century AD to entertain some 15,000 legionnaires. There is more to Óbuda than its Roman heritage, however. Immediately north of Szentlélek tér is **Fő tér**, the old town square, which is small, picturesque and handsomely renovated. In the summer, open-air concerts are held here. The **Zichy Palace**, the striking Baroque building that dominates the square, now houses the **Vasarely Museum** (www.vasarely.hu; Wed–Sun

10am–6pm). It showcases the work of Victor Vasarely, the internationally renowned pioneer of the Op Art Movement, which exploits optical effects, with patterns in brilliant colours.

Standing near the **Imre Varga Museum** (Laktanya utca 7; Tues–Sun 10am–4pm) are whimsical figures with umbrellas – a clue to the collection housed inside. Varga is considered one of Hungary's greatest sculptors, and whether his materials and subject matter are conventional, as in *Umbrellas*, or more offbeat, as with many of his other works, he always remains accessible and popular; he is also well known for designing the Holocaust memorial sculpture outside the Dohány Street Synagogue. Varga died in 2019 aged 96.

The other major museum in the area is the **Kiscelli** (Kiscelli utca 108; www.kiscellimuzeum.hu; Tues–Sun 10am–6pm). You can reach it by taking tram No. 17 from Margaret Bridge to the terminal and then walking uphill towards the Baroque mansion, once a Trinitarian monastery. The building now shelters the Budapest municipal collection of Hungarian art.

BUDA HILLS

The **Buda Hills** ⓭ are a wooded area to the west of Rózsadomb, stretching as far north as Óbuda and as far south as the start of the M7 motorway. On a clear day, strike out on the 20-minute walk or catch any of the several trams or buses that journey to the cogwheel railway terminus, west of Széll Kálmán tér (one of the city's major transport hubs) and opposite the *Hotel Belvedere Budapest*.

The cogwheel railway, which shuttles passengers up to **Széchenyi-hegy**, wends through smart residential housing. At the top, there's a signpost pointing to **Gyermekvasút**, the Children's Railway (see www.gyermekvasut.hu for timetables). This is an 11km (7-mile) narrow-gauge railway run by children, although adults drive the engines and the regulations of the MÁV state railways apply.

If you want to go up the hill when neither the Children's Railway nor the cog railway are operating (the former is closed on Mondays and for periods in mid-winter), take bus No. 21, which runs from Széll Kálmán tér to **Normafa** – a ski resort when there's enough snow. From the bus terminus at Normafa, you can walk, run or cycle through the forest. **János-hegy** is an enjoyable walk of about an hour or so each way through the woods, with plenty of fauna and flora to admire en route.

If you would like to return to town by a different route, there is a chairlift, **Zugliget** (www.bkv.hu/en/zugliget_chairlift_; May–Aug daily 10am–7pm; April and Sept daily 10am–6pm, shorter hours the rest of the year; closed every other Mon for maintenance) that descends to a campsite, from where you catch the No. 155 bus back to Széll Kálmán tér. As you float slowly down the

The Children's Railway is one of a kind

mountainside, you will enjoy some spectacular views over the forest to the spires and rooftops of the city.

At this point, if you want to explore the hills further, there are several places of interest; most can be reached by bus or train. Take bus No. 5 to the home of **Béla Bartók ⓚ**, now preserved as a museum (Bartók Béla Emlékház; www.bartokemlekhaz.hu), at Csalán út 29. The museum is currently closed, but there are piano recitals and concerts in a 120-seat event room at the memorial house and in an adjacent garden most Saturdays; see the website for the full programme.

Hármashatár-hegy (Three Border Hill) is another pleasant spot to relax, hike, picnic and enjoy views of the city. Sometimes, hang-gliding enthusiasts use it as a take-off point. It's reached by going to the terminal on bus No. 65 from Kolosy tér.

The hills also offer rare opportunities for speleology. Some caves are accessible to the public, including **Pálvölgyi barlang** (www.dunaipoly.hu/hu/helyek/bemutatohelyek/pal-volgyi-barlang; Tues–Sun 10am–4pm; guided tours at quarter past every hour, 10.15am–4.15pm) on Szépvölgyi út. It is vast, with about 7km (4.5 miles) explored so far. Some 500 metres (1,640ft) are covered on the hour-long guided tours; the walking is not too difficult, but there is some ladder-climbing so you will need suitable footwear. Nearby, on Pusztaseri út, is **Szemlő-hegyi barlang** (www.dunaipoly.hu/en/places/interpretation-sites/szemlo-hegyi-cave; Wed–Mon 10am–4pm; guided tours on the hour), which has beautiful mineral formations and is sculpted by stalactites and stalagmites.

CROSSING THE DANUBE

Returning now to the city centre, this section takes us down the Danube from north to south. The first bridge reached is the relatively modern **Árpád híd** (híd = bridge), which gives access to the northern end of Margaret Island (Margitsziget, see page 74). At

Chain Bridge

At the grand opening of the Chain Bridge (Széchenyi Lánchíd) it is said that a small boy exclaimed loudly: 'The lions have no tongues!' So embarrassed was the designer, he jumped into the Danube and was never seen again.

the southern end is **Margaret Bridge** ⓯ (Margit híd), which is really two bridges at an angle, with access to the island from the centre. It is the modern replacement of the nineteenth-century version destroyed in World War II and links the Grand Boulevard to Buda.

If Tower Bridge epitomizes London, Brooklyn Bridge symbolizes New York, and the Golden Gate is the pride of San Francisco, Budapest has the landmark **Chain Bridge** ⓰ (Széchenyi Lánchíd). This impressive crossing, inaugurated in 1849, was the first bridge to link Buda and Pest, and one of its initial functions was to enable the Hungarian army of independence to flee from the advancing Austrians. Count István Széchenyi, a great innovator, imported the technology and expertise of Britain's industrial revolution to assist Hungary's own reform programme. An English engineer, William Tierney Clark, designed the Chain Bridge, and its construction was supervised by a Scotsman, Adam Clark (the shared surname is a coincidence; they were not related), after whom the square at the Buda end of the bridge is named.

The bridge has graceful twin arches and is guarded by a pair of massive stone lions at each approach. Don't miss seeing the bridge when it is floodlit at night – it is one of the city's finest sights.

South of the Chain Bridge is the somewhat functional-looking **Elizabeth Bridge** ⓱ (Erzsébet híd), named after the consort of Emperor Franz Josef. The original was destroyed during World War II and was replaced with a suspension bridge (less expensive than rebuilding the original), which opened in 1964.

The next bridge you reach is the green-ironwork **Liberty Bridge** ⓲ (Szabadság híd), which was built for the 1896 Magyar millennium (celebrating the conquest of the Carpathian Basin) and originally called the Franz Josef Bridge. Look for the turul birds perched on golden balls balancing on each pillar (see page 28).

Further south is the functional, 1930s **Petőfi Bridge** and the newest bridge, **Rákóczi híd**, completed in 1995. The bridge is named after an old noble family, but it was formerly called Lágymányosi híd and this is still how it is most commonly referred to.

The Pest riverside offers splendid views of Buda and the hills beyond, and one of the nicest things to do in Budapest is to take tram No. 2, which traces the river's edge. Hop off near Vigadó tér, where people like to stroll, meet friends and enjoy the café

Looking out over the Danube at night

The exquisite Liberty Bridge

terraces. On the railings on **Dunakorzó** (the pedestrianized embankment), look out for the *Little Princess*, a statue of a quaint little girl with a jester's hat. She has shiny golden knees because people touch them for luck. Nearby is a statue of Shakespeare, which was unveiled on 23 April 2003 (exactly 439 years after he was born and 387 years after he died). This is a copy of an original statue by Andor Mészáros, which is in Ballarat, Australia.

PEST

Modern Budapest lies on the east side of the Danube in what was, until 1873, the autonomous city of Pest. With its conglomeration of hotels, museums, government offices, banks, shopping streets, nightclubs, cafés, busy boulevards and handsome Art Nouveau apartment buildings, Pest is where the pulse of the modern capital beats strongest.

THE INNER CITY (BELVÁROS)

In AD 294, the Romans built a fortress on the great expanse of flat plains to the east of the river to make it harder for invaders to establish a foothold near their garrison. They called the place Contra-Aquincum; today, it is the core of the Inner City (Belváros), the shopping and entertainment centre of Budapest.

The focal point of Pest's pedestrian zone is **Váci utca ❿** (pronounced *Vah-tsee oot-sa*), where you can buy clothes, cosmetics, jewellery, art and books. You will also find a cluster of restaurants and cafés.

Váci utca empties north into the shopping square called **Vörösmarty tér**, one of Pest's most popular gathering places. A classic rest stop for residents and visitors alike is **Gerbeaud** (www. gerbeaud.hu), doyen of Budapest's café scene since 1884, and famed for its confectionery and patisserie. The interior is sumptuous, with high ceilings, decorative plasterwork and wooden panelling. Equally popular with visitors is the terrace outside, from where you can watch the world go by. Look out, too, for *Gerbeaud*'s gourmet restaurant, *Onyx* (see page 112), established in 2007, just round the corner on the same block.

Stroll a few yards towards the river and you will come to **Vigadó tér**, a pleasant riverside square with unrivalled views of Castle Hill. Here, you will find craft stalls and any number of buskers. A vibrant café-restaurant fills one side of the square, but the dominant building is the **Pesti Vigadó Theatre** (www.pestivigado.hu). The grand auditorium was renovated in 1980 (its predecessors having perished through war and revolution), but the glorious, mid-nineteenth-century Hungarian-Eastern style facade has survived. The list of performers and conductors who have graced the Vigadó Theatre is a Who's Who of the past 150 years of European classical music: Liszt, Brahms, Wagner, Mahler, Bartók, Prokofiev, Casals, Björling and von Karajan among them.

From Vörösmarty tér, take Deák Ferenc utca to busy **Deák tér**. This is the point where three metro lines meet, so it is an apt place for the tiny **Millennium Underground Museum** ⑳ (Földalatti Vasúti Múzeum; www.bkv.hu/en; Tues–Sun 10am–5pm), located in the Deák tér subway. Here, you can see the train that travelled on Europe's first continental underground railway in 1896.

Also on Deák tér, at No. 4, is the oldest evangelical church in the city and the **National Lutheran Museum** (Evangélikus Országos Múzeum; www.eom.lutheran.hu; Tues–Sun 10am–6pm), charting the history of Protestantism in this largely Catholic country, and containing Martin Luther's will, dated 1542. Almost opposite is the **Tourist Information office** (see page 131). The mustard-coloured building dominating the far side of the square is the **Anker Palace**,

On the terrace at Gerbeaud

a former insurance company headquarters and one of the few structures to escape World War II unscathed.

Walk down Barczy utca, which runs along the back of the Lutheran Church and, on your right, the **Budapest City Hall** fills an entire street. It was built in 1711 as a home for disabled soldiers, served for a time as an army barracks, and became the town hall in 1894. The nineteenth-century, Neoclassical Pest County Hall lies a little further along the same street.

Nearby is Szervita tér, notable for a splendid Art Nouveau mosaic on the gable of the **Turkish Banking House** (Török Bánkház). Now, head south along Petőfi Sándor utca and on your right is the **Paris Arcade** (Párizsi Udvar), built in 1909, with Art Nouveau flourishes and a stained-glass ceiling.

CHURCHES AND UNIVERSITY BUILDINGS

Three fine churches and part of the university complex lie across the busy road (use the underpass). The **Franciscan Church** (Ferenciek templom), built in 1758, stands on the corner of Ferenciek tere. A relief on the side depicts the flood of 1838, which caused massive destruction to the inner city. Continue along Károlyi Mihály utca, past the yellow University Library building on the left. On the opposite corner is the **University Church** (Egyetemi templom), built in 1725–42 by monks of the Order of St Paul, with a rich Baroque interior. Along the quiet street called Szerb utca is the eighteenth-century **Serbian Orthodox Church of St George**. It has an iconostasis – the screen that divides the nave from the sanctuary in Eastern Orthodox churches – with a large number of icons on display.

Kossuth Lajos utca turns into Szabadsajtó út as it approaches the river. On the right-hand side, along Március tér, is the oldest building in Pest, the **Inner City Parish Church** ㉑ (Belvárosi templom), now hemmed into an undignified position by the

Elizabeth Bridge. The soot-covered, Baroque exterior is unremarkable, but the handsome interior is far more interesting. It was founded in the twelfth century, and some Romanesque elements are still visible. So, too, is the influence of the Turks, who turned the church into a mosque and carved a mihrab (prayer niche) on the chancel wall, facing Mecca. Next to the church is all that remains of the ancient Roman defences of Contra-Aquincum – an excavated square with a display of tablets and reliefs from the site.

THE LITTLE BOULEVARD

You won't probably find **Kiskörút** – the so-called Little Boulevard – marked up on a map, but it follows the line of the old city walls and wraps around the district of Belváros. A medieval town grew around

the original Roman defensive post, evolving into a long, narrow strip that is boxed in by the Danube to the west and by defensive walls on the other sides. The city walls were later replaced by three roads (Károly körút, Múzeum körút and Vámház körút), which are now known collectively as Kiskörút. The boulevard stretches right the way from Deák Ferenc tér to the Liberty Bridge. If you want to see the whole strip in comfort, it's best to take a tram (No. 47 or 49). There are several places of interest en route.

Franciscan Church

Central Market Hall

The **Central Market Hall** ㉒ (Nagyvásárcsarnok; Mon 6am–5pm, Tues–Fri until 6pm, Sat until 3pm) is on Vámház körút, by the Szabadság híd (Liberty Bridge), and was built here because the excellent transport links ensured the arrival of fresh produce. The hall was restored in 1996, and it now has a supermarket on the lower level, while the ground floor sells vegetables, fruit, spices, meat and dairy produce, and there are handicrafts upstairs. There's a busy self-service café, the **Fakanál étterem** (www.fakanaletterem.hu), selling large helpings of good, fresh Hungarian food at modest prices. It's a friendly, homely place with a fiddler providing suitable musical accompaniment.

The boulevard continues through Kálvin tér, with the statue of Calvin dwarfed by coloured café umbrellas, to Múzeum körút, dominated by the **Hungarian National Museum** ㉓ (Magyar Nemzeti Múzeum; www.mnm.hu; Tues–Sun 10am–6pm). It was Hungary's first public collection and it remains the country's largest museum. It was built in 1846 in Neoclassical style with Corinthian columns and a sculpted pediment. Inside, amid monumental architectural and ornamental details, the whole story of Hungary unfolds – from the prehistoric history of the Carpathian Basin right up to the twenty-first century. On display are prehistoric remains, ancient jewellery and tools, Roman mosaics, a seventeenth-century Turkish tent fitted out with grand carpets,

Eiffel in Budapest

The vast Budapest Central Market Hall was designed and erected by the firm of Gustave Eiffel, who built the iconic Eiffel Tower in Paris – so take note of the distinctive ironwork.

a Baroque library, and some royal regalia – although the crown, orb, sceptre and sword are now displayed in the Houses of Parliament (see page 59).

On Rákóczi út (just off Múzeum körút), is the celebrated **Uránia cinema** (Uránia Nemzeti Filmszínház; www.urania-nf.hu). A mix of Venetian Gothic and Moorish styles, it was built in 1895, and was restored in 2002. It shows Hungarian and European arthouse films and some international blockbusters; it is also a centre for film festivals and other cultural events.

Jewish Budapest

Back on the Little Boulevard, at the start of **Dohány utca** (Tobacco Street), you can't miss the enormous synagogue in flamboyant, Byzantine-Moorish style. The **Great Synagogue** ㉔ (Nagy Zsinagóga; Sun–Thurs 10am–6pm, Fri until 4pm, with exceptions) dates from the mid-nineteenth century, and is crowned by two onion-shaped copper domes. Before World War II, there were 125 synagogues in Budapest. This one is claimed to be the largest in Europe (the second largest in the world, after one in New York) and can accommodate up to 3000 people. The great organ has been played by Liszt and Saint-Saens. The synagogue suffered severe war damage and was renovated in the 1990s.

Adjacent to the synagogue, on the site of a house where the founder of Modern Zionism, Theodore Herzl, was born in 1860, is the **Jewish Museum** (Zsidó Múzeum; Dohány utca 2; www.milev.hu; same hours as Synagogue). It contains artefacts and treasures relating to the city's community, as well as an exhibit about the

Holocaust in Hungary. In a courtyard is the Raoul Wallenberg memorial garden, with a metal weeping willow tree by sculptor Imre Varga. Each leaf bears the name of one of the Budapest families who perished in the Holocaust. The site lies above the mass graves of Jews who were executed by the fascist Arrow Cross Government that was installed by the Nazis in 1944–5.

Despite the tragic events memorialized here, a visit to the Jewish Quarter is inspiring. The area is thriving; there are about 80,000 Jewish residents, the children attend Jewish schools, and Yiddish is studied at the University of Budapest. The district has also emerged as a lively nightlife hotspot, with a crop of fashionable bars springing up.

The area surrounding the Great Synagogue (between Király utca and Wesselényi utca) was the heart of the old Jewish community.

The monumental interior of the Hungarian National Museum

The junction of Rumbach Sebestyén utca and Dob utca was the position of the old entrance to the ghetto.

LEOPOLD TOWN

Bounded by József Attila utca to the south and by Bajcsy-Zsilinszky út to the east, **Leopold Town** (Lipótváros) lies just north of the inner city. Directly opposite the approach to the Chain Bridge is Roosevelt tér, a square named after the former US president. Gresham Palace, the grand Art Nouveau building facing the square, was built in 1907 for an insurance company. It is now the *Four Seasons Gresham Palace*, an elegant hotel. The statue in the centre of Roosevelt Square is of Ferenc Deák, who brokered the Compromise with Austria in 1867 (see page 20).

Remembering Holocaust victims at the Great Synagogue

Basilica of St Stephen

The **Basilica of St Stephen** ㉕ (Szent István Bazilika; www.bazilika.biz; Mon 9am–4.30pm, Tues–Sat 9am–5.45pm, Sun 1–5.45pm) is three blocks east of Roosevelt tér, and its 96-metre (315ft) dome dominates the skyline. Completed in 1905, after half a century of work, it is the largest church in Budapest; it can hold 8500 people, and is often full to capacity. Before going inside, make the climb (or take the lift) up to the dome for Pest's highest viewpoint (equal in height to the dome of London's Houses of Parliament). In a reliquary in a rear chapel is the Szent Jobb (Holy Right), the much-revered, somewhat macabre mummified right hand of St Stephen.

Szabadság tér (Liberty Square), a short walk to the north, is home to what is arguably Pest's finest architectural ensemble. At the centre is an obelisk dedicated to the Soviet troops who fell in the city, but the monumental buildings surrounding the square are far more impressive. The lemon-hued Art Nouveau building at No. 12 is now the American Embassy. South of the embassy is the **Hungarian National Bank** and former **Postal Savings Bank** building, a lovely example of Secessionist (Art Nouveau) architecture. Built in 1901, it is decorated with glazed ceramic tiles and floral mosaics. Across the square is the former Stock Exchange. It is an eclectic-style building by Ignác Alpár, who also designed the National Bank. In the film version of *Evita* it served as the Argentine presidential building, the Casa Rosada.

Houses of Parliament and Ethnographic Museum

The great dome of the **Houses of Parliament** ㉖ (Országház), where the national government holds its sessions, is clearly visible from the square. The Parliament, designed by Imre Steindl, was built between 1885 and 1904 to symbolize the grandeur of the Austro-Hungarian Empire. When completed, it was the largest parliament building in the world: 268 metres (880ft) long, with

Parliament viewed from across the Danube

691 rooms, and 29 staircases. The architect clearly had London's Houses of Parliament in mind, emulating the neo-Gothic arches and turrets, and even its early form of air conditioning – involving blocks of ice and an intricate network of ventilation shafts. Visitors are admitted on guided tours to certain parts of the building when Parliament is not in session. Tours begin to the right of the main stairs and enter through the grandiose central stairway to a splendid, 16-sided domed hall, then into the lobby, and finally into the principal debating chamber of the Upper House (www.parlament.hu; visitor centre: May–Oct daily 8am–6pm; Nov–March daily 8am–4pm; April Mon–Thurs 8am–4pm, Fri–Sun 8am–6pm).

Located just opposite the Houses of Parliament is the city's **Ethnographic Museum** (Néprajzi Múzeum; www.neprajz.hu; Tues–Sun 10am–6pm, sometimes until 8pm; check website for precise opening hours). Built in 1893 to house the Supreme Court of Justice, it is worth a visit for the palatial interior alone. But it is also a fine museum, with displays on Hungarian folk art, crafts, rural life and dress. A video, showing how people used to dress in wonderfully complex embroidered layers, is fascinating, and many exhibits are shown next to vintage photographs showing similar objects *in situ*. The temporary exhibitions are also usually excellent.

The eternal flame located outside the Parliament Building was lit in 1996, the fortieth anniversary of the 1956 Hungarian revolution. The statue of **Imre Nagy**, in an overcoat and hat, stands gazing into the flame. He was the prime minister executed for his part in the revolution.

ANDRÁSSY ÚT

Modelled on the Champs-Elysées in Paris, **Andrássy út** ㉗ was driven straight through the city in the 1870s. Almost 2.5km (1-mile) long, it connects the inner city to Városliget, the City Park (see page 68). The avenue is lined with some of Budapest's finest

THE CROWN JEWELS

The crown jewels (St Stephen's crown, orb, sceptre and sword) were installed in Parliament on 1 January 2000, the 1000th anniversary of the coronation of King Stephen. They had previously been housed in the Hungarian National Museum, and the move was controversial as it was seen as an attempt to alter the crown's status from museum relic to living icon: an embodiment of the sovereignty of Hungary. The famous crown is romantically associated with St Stephen, but is actually of a slightly later date (the lower half is eleventh century, the upper, twelfth century). The treasures have had a history of being stolen, grabbed, pawned, seized, buried or lost, and of reappearing. After World War II, they ended up in Fort Knox and were restored to Hungary in 1978.

architecture, and its palaces and apartment buildings are gradually being restored. The elegance of the leafy avenue belies the prosaic nature of its former names – it has been known variously as Népköztársaság útja (People's Republic Avenue), Sugár út (Radial Road) and even, to the disgust of Budapestis, as Stalin út.

Located at No. 22 is the grand, neo-Renaissance **Hungarian State Opera House** (Magyar Állami Operaház; www.opera.hu; guided tours in English daily at 1.30pm, 3pm and 4.30pm along with tours in several languages, subject to performances; other languages available on request). Completed in 1884 by Miklós Ybl, this is the most admired building on the avenue. Its Italianate style and restrained proportions complement its surroundings exquisitely. The opulent gilt and marble interior is splendid and the architecture, atmosphere and acoustics rank among the very finest in Europe.

The building reopened to much fanfare in early 2022 after being closed for almost five years for extensive renovations, particularly to the stage itself. If you are an opera lover and are keen to catch a performance, you will find that tickets are surprisingly reasonable in price.

The artistic theme continues at **Dreschler House**, an Art Nouveau building just across the street and once home to the State Ballet. Down the small street to the right is the **New Theatre** (Új Színház; Paulay Ede utca 35; www.ujszinhaz.hu), topped by a colourful piece of geometric Art Nouveau embellishment.

No. 29 Andrássy út should not be overlooked. It is **Művész kávéház** (www.muveszkavehaz.com), purveyors of fine confectionery since 1887, the *Artist Café* and a coffeehouse where you can get a coffee and a pastry in the most elegant surroundings.

The pedestrian-only precinct called **Liszt Ferenc tér** holds a clutch of restaurants and chic cafés. In the middle is a modern statue of Liszt, who is portrayed in action, almost a caricature,

The opulent Opera House

with flailing hands and wild, windswept hair. The **Liszt Academy of Music** (Zeneakadémia; www.zeneakademia.hu), completed in 1907, is at the end of the precinct. This Art Nouveau gem has a handsome facade, lobby and interior. Even if you're not attending a concert, it's usually quite easy to look inside.

Cross the busy junction of Oktogon, and three streets north at Vörösmarty utca 35 you will find the **Franz Liszt Memorial Museum** (Liszt Ference Emlékmúzeum; www.lisztmuseum.hu; Mon–Fri 10am–6pm, Sat 9am–5pm). This delightful collection of pianos, memorabilia and period furnishings is displayed in an apartment where the composer once lived.

Back on Andrássy út, at No. 60, almost opposite the Liszt Museum is the **House of Terror ㉘** (Terror Háza; www.terrorhaza. hu; Tues–Sun 10am–6pm). You can't miss it: the word 'terror' is cut out from an awning around the roof, and the sun shines through, projecting the word onto the side of the grey building. Allied to

Bronze statue of the composer Franz Liszt

Hitler, the Hungarian Arrow Cross Party was in large part responsible for rounding up Jews during World War II, before sending them to the death camps. This building was their headquarters – though after the war, it became, in turn, that of the communist secret police. Today, it isn't so much a museum dispassionately displaying artefacts, but a centre documenting the harshness of totalitarianism. It concludes by charting the end of the Soviet era, the re-burial of Nagy, the Pope's visit and the fact that the perpetrators of so much suffering were never brought to justice. It remains controversial, as it has revealed familial links of current politicians with their communist predecessors or even with members of the secret police.

On the opposite side of Andrássy út, at No. 69, is the **Puppet Theatre** (Babszinház;www.budapestbabszinhaz.hu), one of the largest of its kind, which puts on excellent puppet performances, popular with adults and children alike.

As Andrássy út edges closer to the City Park, the villas and mansions in garden settings get noticeably grander. Many of them now house embassies. **Kodály körönd** (a square named after Hungarian composer, Zoltán Kodály) is a splendid ensemble, its curving facades decorated with classical figures and inlaid motifs. In an apartment at No. 1 is an archive and museum devoted to the composer, **Zoltán Kodály Memorial Museum and Archives**

(Kodály Zoltán Emlékmúzeum és Archívum; www.kodaly.hu; visits by appointment only).

At Andrássy út 103 is the **Ferenc Hopp Museum of Asiatic Arts** (Hopp Ferenc Kelet-Ázsiai Művészeti Múzeum; www.hopp museum.hu; Tues–Sun 10am–6pm). Hopp was a businessman who, by the time of his death in 1919, had amassed a vast collection of pieces. Some 20,000 items are on display.

The **György Ráth Villa** (Ráth György-villa; www.imm.hu; Tues–Sun 10am–6pm), which displays the personal treasures of the first director of the city's Museum of Applied Arts, lies just to the south, in a handsome Art Nouveau villa. Nearby, the second floor of a villa at Benczúr utca 27 is now home to the **Postal Museum** (Postamúzeum; www.postamuzeum.hu; Tues–Sun 10am–6pm; closes at 4pm in winter). It has an interesting collection of colourful postal memorabilia and postal vehicles, and the building itself – a magnificent nineteenth-century palace – is an attraction as well.

FRANZ LISZT

Franz (Ferenc) Liszt, composer and pianist, was born in 1811 in Raiding, Hungary, where his father, an amateur musician, was steward to the Esterházy family. As a boy, Liszt studied in Vienna, then went to Paris, where he was idolized, and mixed with the most celebrated writers and artists of his day. He later worked in Weimar, Rome and Budapest, where he became president of the Academy of Music. Liszt was a complex man; torn between the adulation of audiences, the pleasures of fashionable society – including the company of beautiful women – and the desire for isolation in which to compose great works, he vacillated between the two worlds. In the latter part of his life he became religious and took minor orders in the church. He died in Bayreuth in 1886.

HEROES' SQUARE

Andrássy út ends in a burst of pomp at **Heroes' Square** ㉙ (Hősök tere), a large open space focussed around the **Millennium Monument**, built on the 1000th anniversary of the Magyar settlement of the region. The 36-metre (118ft) column supports the figure of the Archangel Gabriel who, according to legend, appeared to St Stephen in a dream and offered him the crown of Hungary. Around the pedestal sit Prince Árpád and the Magyar chiefs on horseback, while flanking the column is a semi-circular colonnade with statues of historical figures, starting with King Stephen. In front of the statuary is the Tomb of the Unknown Soldier. The communist-era demonstrations that took place here have given way to youthful skateboarders who hang out at the base of the monument and bob and weave through cones around the square.

Squaring up to one another across Heroes' Square are two large neoclassical edifices that are near mirror images of each other. On the right is the **Műcsarnok** (Palace of Art; www.mucsarnok. hu; Tues–Wed and Fri–Sun 10am–6pm, Thurs noon–8pm), which mounts high-quality temporary exhibitions of work by contemporary Hungarian and foreign artists, and also has a fine bookstore. Outside, a splendid pediment crowns the building with a mosaic of St Stephen in his role as patron saint of the arts.

Located just behind Műcsarnok is one of the world's biggest hourglasses: **Timewheel** was unveiled at midnight on 30 April to mark Hungary's entry to the European Union. As the name suggests, it's a huge wheel, 8 metres (26ft) in diameter, and weighs 40 tonnes. Made of Indian granite carved in Italy and Swiss steel, the clock turns once a year, in a half circle, setting the sand running anew, to usher in the new year.

Opposite the Műcsarnok is the **Museum of Fine Arts** ㉚ (Szépművészeti Múzeum; www.mfab.hu; Tues–Sun 10am–6pm)

Heroes' Square centres around the Millennium Monument

holding the city's most highly regarded and wide-ranging collection. It begins chronologically with Greek, Roman and Egyptian treasures but the most significant section is that of European painting from 1300–1800.

There are around 2500 masterpieces, of which some 800 are on show at any one time. Italian, Dutch, German and Spanish schools are all superbly represented. The latter is particularly notable, constituting one of the best collections of Spanish Old Masters outside Spain, with paintings by El Greco, Goya and others.

There are also rooms dedicated to British, French and Flemish artists. The nineteenth- to twentieth-century collection includes a treasure trove of French Impressionist and Post-Impressionist artists such as Cézanne, Pissarro, Monet, Gauguin and Renoir. Leonardo da Vinci is featured in the prints and drawings sections, and the museum also possesses a bronze horseman by the great artist.

Museum of Fine Arts

CITY PARK

Beyond Heroes' Square is the **City Park** ❸ (Városliget), a large green space where Budapestis stroll, picnic, hire boats and family-sized pedal-cars, go to the zoo and visit museums. The park, which covers some 100 hectares (250 acres), began to evolve in the early nineteenth century, although many of the present amenities were added during preparations for the Magyar Millennium festivities of 1896. Sir Winston Churchill and George Washington are represented among the statues.

Across the bridge over the boating lake, which doubles as an ice-skating rink in winter, lies the **Vajdahunyad Castle** ❸ (Vajdahunyad vára). It was conceived as a temporary building for the Millennium Exhibition in 1896, but proved so popular that it was rebuilt in permanent form. It reproduces part of the exterior of the fairy-tale Hunyadi Castle in Transylvania, hence the name, but it is also a catalogue of Hungarian architectural history – Gothic,

Romanesque, baroque – it's all here. Inside the castle is the **Museum of Hungarian Agriculture** (Mezőgazdasági Múzeum; www.mmgm.hu; Tues–Sun 10am–5pm), housing a comprehensive collection illustrating the history of Hungarian horse-breeding, hunting, fishing and farming. If you want to see the castle at its best, return at night, when it is beautifully illuminated.

Also within the castle precinct is a Catholic church, the **Ják Chapel**, with a Romanesque portal and cloisters (modelled on genuinely old churches elsewhere in Hungary). One of the city's favourite statues is seated just out front: *Anonymous* depicts the medieval chronicler who gave Hungary its first written records. The scribe's face is hidden inside the cowl of his habit; aspiring writers seek inspiration by touching his pen.

Also within the park are the zoo, a spa complex, a circus and an amusement park. In the northeast corner of the area is the **Holnemvolt Park** (Holnemvolt Vár; www.zoobudapest.com/ ezt-latnod-kell/kiallitasok/ holnemvolt-var; Mon–Fri 9am–5.30pm, Sat–Sun 9am– 6pm), a funfair-style amusement park for children. It is now part of the zoo, so you will also find numerous animal-petting sites here and you can watch a parrot parade or ride a pony. A carousel dating from 1906, the wooden roller coaster opened in 1922 and the

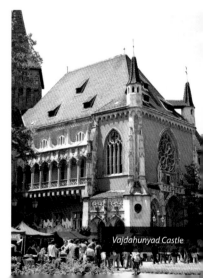
Vajdahunyad Castle

1912-built cave railway have been taken over from the Vidám Amusement Park, which operated here for 175 years until 2013. Next door to the amusement park is the **Municipal Grand Circus** (Fővárosi Nagycirkusz; www.fnc.hu; shows Wed–Sun 3pm, also Sat–Sun 11am; some later shows, see website for full timetable), with strongmen, acrobats and clowns.

In the northwest corner of the park, the **Zoo** ③③ (Állatkert; www.zoobudapest.com; Mon–Fri 9am–6pm, Sat and Sun 9am–7pm, but times can vary so check online), one of the oldest in the world (1866), welcomes visitors through an Art Nouveau entrance decorated with polar bears and elephants. The Elephant House is a handsome construction with a tall minaret, while the Palm House is the largest tropical hall in Central Europe. Next to the zoo is *Gundel* (see page 110), a fine restaurant that is legendary in Hungarian culinary circles.

Also in the northwest corner is the **Széchenyi Baths** ③④ (Széchenyi fürdő; www.szechenyibath.hu; Mon, Wed and Thurs 7am–7pm, Tues and Fri 8am–8pm, Sat and Sun 9am–8pm). One of the largest therapeutic bath complexes in Europe, it provides year-round open-air swimming, at a constant temperature of 27˚C (81˚F), in beautiful surroundings. The neo-Baroque buildings,

HUNGARIAN PLAYING CARDS

Not hearts, diamonds, clubs and spades but leaves, bells, acorns and hearts: Hungary has its own style of playing cards, designed in Budapest in 1830 by Jószef Schneider, a prominent manufacturer of cards. The most popular are 'Tell cards' which feature characters from the tales about the legendary Swiss patriot, William Tell. There are other designs too: royal personages of the Austro-Hungarian monarchy and medieval heroes are also commonly found.

bright yellow and topped by a series of green domes, opened in 1881. Inside the pool area, surrounded by ivy-clad walls and sumptuous statuary, groups of men stand up to their chests in warm water amid the steam, concentrating intently on games of chess (the chess boards form part of the small jetties that protrude into the pool).

The Secessionist-style Museum of Applied Arts

Anybody keen on architecture should keep their eyes peeled near City Park for splendid examples of Art Nouveau. One unusually shaped building is home to the **National Association for the Blind** (Hermina út 47). Another, slightly more out of the way, is the **Geology Institute** (Stefánia út 14; www.mbfsz.gov.hu/en/home), a marvellous structure adorned by blue tiles and statues of Atlas supporting globes. There is a small geological museum inside.

THE GREAT BOULEVARD

The bustling **Great Boulevard** (Nagykörút) forms a long, sweeping arc from Margaret Bridge to the Petőfi Bridge. It doesn't appear on the map because it has five different names along its 3km (2-mile) length: Szent István körút, Teréz körút, Erzsébet körút, Jószef körút and Ferenc körút. The city planners approved the project and pushed it through for the Magyar Millennium year of 1896.

The boat moored close to the Petőfi bridge, the **A38** (www.a38. hu; restaurant: Mon–Fri 10am–10pm, Sat 4–10pm) is a hip club and restaurant, which also hosts many cultural events, from the Asian Dub Foundation to Klezmer music. The name A38 refers to its former life as an Ukranian stone carrier, **Artemorszk 38**.

The architectural big-hitter on the Great Boulevard is the **Museum of Applied Arts** 35 (Iparmũvészeti Múzeum; www.imm. hu; temporarily closed at the time of writing), just off Ferenc körút at Nos 33–37 Üllõi út. The splendid Secessionist exterior incorporates Hungarian folk art and majolica tiles. Huge green cupolas, small spiky towers, a majolica lantern and a bright green-and-gold tiled roof crown the edifice. The museum's architect, Ödön Lechner (who also built the Postal Savings Bank in Leopold Town), is seen as the greatest exponent of this Magyar style.

The interior is just as remarkable: Hungarian with strong Moorish and even Mughal influences. Shimmering white arches, balconies

Chess at Széchenyi Baths

and swirling staircases sweep up to a fine Art Nouveau skylight. The main hall is covered by a great expanse of glass supported by an iron frame, and ferns and potted plants around the hall create a kind of winter garden. A fascinating permanent exhibition, showing the progress of arts and crafts techniques from the twelfth century, is augmented by temporary exhibitions on more specialized subjects. There are striking examples of work in a variety of media – textiles, ceramics, metalwork, leather and wood. The section on Art Nouveau from across the world is particularly interesting.

HOLOCAUST MEMORIAL CENTRE

Across Ferenc körút, further up Üllői utca is Páva utca, the location of the **Holocaust Memorial Centre** (Holokauszt Emlékközpont; www.hdke.hu; Tues–Sun 10am–6pm). Security is tight at the centre, which opened on 16 April 2004, the sixtieth anniversary of the Hungarian Holocaust. The synagogue originally on the site has been restored, and new wings, designed by István Mányi, have been added. The centre has permanent exhibitions as well as being a memorial and an education and research centre. There is a wall on which the names of the victims are recorded.

AN HISTORIC CAFÉ AND A PANORAMIC VIEW

Just beyond Erzsébet körút, at Hársfa utca 47, the **Stamp Museum** (Bélyeg Múzeum; www.belyeg-muzeum.hu; Tues–Sun 10am–6pm)

The Holocaust

The Hungarian Holocaust was the largest and fastest deportation of all: in just 56 days, some 437,402 Jewish citizens were deported, all but 15,000 to Dr Mengele at Auschwitz. A third of the victims of Auschwitz were Hungarian citizens. In all, somewhere between 450,000 and 600,000 Hungarians perished.

contains every stamp issued by Hungary since 1871. The collection, comprising thirteen million items, includes some interesting misprints, such as an upside-down Madonna and child.

Teréz körút and Erzsébet körút have traditionally been centres of Budapest's cultural scene, as well as its commercial life. At the junction of Erzsébet körút and Dohány utca is the **New York Café** ㊱ (www.newyorkcafe.hu), with its glorious neo-Baroque interior. The café's artistic heyday was at the turn of the nineteenth century, followed by a revival in the 1930s; however, it suffered wartime damage and was rammed by a tank in 1956. During the socialist period, the place was reputed to have had the slowest, most disagreeable staff in Budapest. Things couldn't be more different today, with a professionalism and quality that give every customer a real taste of the high life.

Further along, where Teréz körút intersects with Váci utca, is Nyugati railway station – another of Gustave Eiffel's creations. The modern building next door is the Westend Shopping Centre (www.westend.hu), which has all the big-brand retailers, as well as housing a multiplex cinema.

MARGARET ISLAND

Walk onto **Margaret Island** ㊲ (Margitsziget) from the tram stop on Margaret Bridge, and you'll be greeted by the centenary monument and fountain by István Kiss, unveiled in 1972 for the centenary of the union of Buda and Pest. Visitors enjoy the thermal facilities and treatments offered at two hotels on the island; locals also come to walk, bike, play tennis and eat picnics, and, on sunny afternoons, enjoy the enormous outdoor **Palatinus Baths** complex, with thermal pools and a wave pool (Palatinus Strandfürdő; www.palatinus strand.hu; daily 9am–7pm). A beautiful rose garden blooms in front of the baths and nearby is an open-air stage.

Margaret Island is 2km (1.25 miles) long and only a few hundred metres/yards at the widest point. Many of its 10,000 trees are now more than a century old, and large areas of the island have been landscaped. To preserve the island's peace and quiet, cars are prohibited, which comes as a pleasant relief if you are looking for a tranquil break from the city.

The New York Café

Alongside a landmark octagonal water tower (Víztorony; www.margitszigetiszinhaz.hu; Tues–Fri noon–6pm, Sat and Sun 10am–6pm), which offers a splendid view of the island, is an open-air theatre, where concerts, opera and ballet performances are presented in the summer. Nearby are the ruins of a thirteenth-century **Dominican Convent** founded by King Béla IV. The king enrolled his 11-year-old daughter, Margit, at the convent in fulfilment of a vow he made if he survived the Mongol invasion. Princess (later St) Margit remained on the island for the rest of her life, and a marble plaque marks her burial place.

CITY OUTSKIRTS

STATUE AND RAIL HERITAGE PARKS

The **Memento Park** ❸ (Szoborpark Múzeum; www.mementopark.hu; Mon–Fri 10am–5pm, Sat and Sun 10am–6pm) is a slightly surreal park where some of the monumental statues once imposed by the communist regime on the streets of Budapest are displayed. Rather than see them destroyed, the authorities decided to put them here, in a suburban setting. Giant socialist-realist figures of Lenin and anonymous worker heroes strut against the backdrop of newly built homes.

There is a direct bus transfer to the park every day at 11am (Nov–March Sat–Mon only). The bus leaves from Deák tér in the centre of Pest (go to the bus stop with the Memento Park timetable). You can buy your ticket on board; the return ticket price includes entry to the park. The round trip takes about two and a half hours.

Train aficionados should love the **Hungarian Railway Museum** (Magyar Vasúttörténeti Park; www.vasuttortenetipark.hu; Tues–Fri and Sat 10am–6pm), designed as an interactive space dedicated to trains and railways. The best way to get there is to make the 15-minute journey on the vintage shuttle train called the *különvonat* from Nyugati railway station. This service runs from early April to late October, during park opening hours. The park has about 70 vintage steam locomotives and coaches, and a working rotating loading dock. The museum also organizes trips on steam trains elsewhere in Hungary.

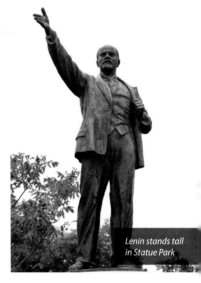

Lenin stands tall in Statue Park

EXCURSIONS

A short distance north of Budapest, the Danube dramatically alters its easterly course for a southern tack. The prosaic name of this extraordinary region is Dunakanyar, meaning the Danube Bend. Here, the river is at its most alluring, the countryside lush and unspoiled, and there are delightful historic towns to explore. **Szentendre**, **Visegrád** and **Ezstergom** can be visited in one trip. If you fancy venturing further afield, you could take a trip to **Lake Balaton** – Hungary's seaside; to the Puszta, the Great Plain; or even up the Danube to Vienna (it takes five hours and hydrofoils ply the route daily).

SZENTENDRE

Szentendre is a honey-pot with numerous souvenir and art and craft shops and stalls. It's known for its churches, artists' colony and many small museums and galleries (close to 100 in total). Tourinform at Dumtsa J. utca 22 will provide you with details. The easiest way to reach the town, about 20km (12 miles) from the city, is by HÉV suburban railway from Batthyány tér in Buda. In summer, boats make a five-hour journey all the way from Budapest to Esztergom, stopping en route at Szentendre and Visegrád.

Serbian refugees twice settled in Szentendre in the wake of Turkish invasions, first in the late thirteenth century, and again in 1690. On the latter occasion, around 8000 Serbs settled, and brought their religion, art, architecture and commercial acumen with them. These days, the area between Budapest and Szentendre is mainly commuting country.

The majestic hillside Serbian church is the town's most prominent landmark. **Fő tér** is a picture-postcard square that remains pretty much as it was in the eighteenth century, lined with houses that once belonged to wealthy burghers. The Serbian community erected the iron rococo memorial cross in the centre of the plaza in 1763, in gratitude for being spared by the plague.

The rust-red, eighteenth-century **Serbian Orthodox Church** (Belgrád székesegyház) perched on the hill is only open for services, but within its grounds is the excellent **Collection of Serbian Ecclesiastical Art**, displaying precious carvings, icons and manuscripts. The oldest church in the town lies just above here on the summit, affording a perfect vantage point from which to peer down into the tiny gardens and courtyards, and across the sea of clay rooftops.

SKANSEN

An unusual attraction can be found 4km (2 miles) from Szentendre – **Skansen**, the **Hungarian Open Air Museum** (Szabadtéri Néprajzi Múzeum; www.skanzen.hu; summer Tues–Sun 10am– 5pm, closed in winter). Skansen, the name of the original Swedish village museum, has been naturalized into Hungarian. Catch the No. 7 bus departing from the terminal next to the hév station. The 46-hectare (115-acre) museum site contains villages of genuine houses, churches, mills, farm buildings, workshops and smithies, dating mostly from the late-eighteenth to the early twentieth century, and gathered from across Hungary. Live demonstrations by craftspeople bring to life village traditions.

VISEGRÁD

Upstream, where the Danube truly bends, lies **Visegrád** (meaning 'High Castle'), which is accessible by boat or bus from Szentendre. The finest place to enjoy the panoramic views – reminiscent of the countryside of the Rhine – is the citadel, high on a hill above the ruins of the old palace of Visegrád.

The strategic value of a site commanding the river bend was appreciated as early as the fourth century, when the Romans built a fort here. In the fourteenth century, the Angevin kings of Hungary built a **palace** on the site, each monarch adding new rooms and piling on opulence until the building covered an area now estimated at some 18 hectares (45 acres). When King Mátyás lived here, the palace was famous throughout Europe as an 'earthly paradise'. Between 1462 and

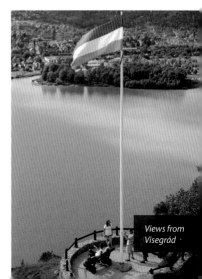

Views from Visegrád

1475, Vlad the Impaler (on whom the Dracula legend was partly based) was held prisoner here.

Like Buda Castle, the palace of Visegrád fell into ruin during the Turkish occupation (although it was not captured and destroyed by the Turks) and was eventually forgotten. Excavations began in 1930; part of the main building has been unearthed and certain sections have been rebuilt (using materials that are obviously new, to differentiate these sections from the original ones). Among the best of the discoveries are the superb Hercules Fountain (a rare vestige of Hungarian Renaissance architecture), the vaulted galleries of the Court of Honour, and the restored Lion's Fountain. The hexagonal tower on the hillside is known as the Tower of Solomon. Topping it all is the **citadel** (Visegrádi Fellegvár; May–Sept daily 9am–6pm; March–April, Oct daily 9am–5pm; Nov daily 9am–4pm; Dec–Feb Fri–Sun 10am–4pm), once considered so impregnable that the Hungarian crown jewels were kept here. The Lower Castle complex is now home to the King Matthias Museum (Mátyás Király Múzeum; Tues–Sun 9am–5pm; Solomon Tower May–Sept Wed–Sun 9am–5pm; historical park March–Oct Tues–Sun 10am–6pm).

ESZTERGOM

Esztergom, a further 20km (12 miles) upriver, lacks the picturesque charm (and the tourists) of Szentendre, but is historically important. It is linked by hydrofoil to Budapest, and by boat or bus to Szentendre and Visegrád. Take the boat if you have a couple of hours to spare; the Danube's most scenic stretch lies between Visegrád and Esztergom. King Stephen was born in Esztergom, which was then the capital of Hungary. The town remains the religious centre of the country and has the largest church in the land. The massive **basilica** (Esztergomi Bazilika; www.bazilika-esztergom.hu; church: daily 8am–7pm; for treasury, crypt and tower, hours vary greatly so check online) stands on the site of an eleventh-century church where Stephen was crowned in 1000. That church was destroyed in battle against the Turks. The only atmospheric part of the current building is the rather spooky crypt.

The most valuable part of the basilica is the red-marble side chapel called the **Bakócz-kápolna** – a pure example of Italian Renaissance. Built in the sixteenth century, the chapel, salvaged from the ruins around it and reassembled in the nineteenth century, is all that survives of the original basilica. A highlight of the basilica is the **treasury**, which contains Hungary's richest collection of religious objects. A climb up the tower takes you from priceless treasures to spectacular views; on clear days you can also see all the way to Slovakia.

Alongside the basilica are the remains of a medieval royal palace – excavated and restored to form the **Castle Museum** (Vármúzeuma; www.varmegom.hu; Tues–Sun: April–Oct 10am–6pm; Nov–March 10am–4pm). Among the highlights are St Stephen's Hall, the frescoed Hall of Virtues, and the twelfth-century Royal Chapel. The most interesting collection in Esztergom lies at the foot of Basilica Hill, on the riverside. The **Christian Museum** (Keresztény Múzeum; www.keresztenymuzeum.hu; Tues–Sun 10am–6pm) is one of the best museums of religious art in the country. Covering the Gothic and

The imposing
Esztergom basilica

Renaissance periods from the thirteenth to the sixteenth centuries, it has a number of excellent fourteenth- and fifteenth-century Italian paintings. Also notable is the fifteenth-century coffin of Garamszentbenedek – an intricately carved and painted devotional vehicle, once paraded through the streets at Easter.

LAKE BALATON

Hungary has no coastline so **Lake Balaton** is the next best thing. This massive freshwater lake – at 77km (48 miles) across, with an area of nearly 600 sq km (230 sq miles) it is the largest lake in central and western Europe – is surrounded by verdant hills, orchards, vineyards and historic villages. The northwestern tip of Balaton lies about 100km (62 miles) from Budapest. In winter, the lake freezes over completely, while in summer the shallow water warms quickly, but is subject to wind-driven waves; when a storm blows up even the ferries call it a day. The mildly alkaline water (considered good for the health) attracts swimmers by the thousands. Many holidaymakers avail themselves of the services of local medicinal baths, spas and wellness hotels. On the north shore, **Balatonfüred** has been a spa since Roman times, and is one of the lake's liveliest resorts.

Other attractive parts of the lake include the **Tihany peninsula**, which has National Park status, and Badacsony – an important wine region. The latter is fascinating because of its volcanic past, which is evident as soon as you see the conical hills. Mt Badacsony, the central basalt peak and, at 437 metres (1,434ft), the largest of the extinct volcanoes, is invariably described as 'coffin-shaped'.

Keszthely (pronounced 'kest-hey') is the site of the Festetics family's palace (www.helikonkastely.hu; base hours Tues–Sun 10am–5pm, sometimes longer; check website for details), one of Hungary's most important Baroque monuments. The highlight is the Helikon library, claimed to be the grandest in the country.

Continuing out of Keszthely to the southwest on Highway 71, you reach another good historical collection. The **Balaton Museum** (www.balatonimuzeum.hu; Tues–Sun 9am–5pm, but times vary so check online) portrays the story of the settlement of the lake and the development of its people, including their agricultural and fishing practices, and the lake's flora and fauna.

Near the southwest corner of the lake, **Kis-Balaton** (Little Balaton), a marshy National Reserve, is noted for its rare birdlife. Observation towers are provided for birdwatchers.

The south shore, strung with waterside resorts, is popular among holidaymakers. The largest town is **Siófok**, which has an attractive beach and lively nightlife. Pleasure craft depart from the large harbour, but the most appealing stretch of waterfront is to be found in the gardens immediately east of the port.

Tihany, on Lake Balaton

The opulent surroundings of the Gellért Hotel Baths

THINGS TO DO

SPAS AND BATHS

You don't have to be suffering from a particular ailment to benefit from spa treatment, and there's nothing wrong with a little pampering when you are on holiday (or, indeed, at any time). In Hungary, so-called health and wellness hotels and centres are major attractions. The centres provide saunas and steam baths, alternative therapies, sport and exercise, gastronomy, serious relaxation and a staggering number of beauty and aesthetic treatments. Some of them also offer dentistry and cosmetic surgery. Even shopping centres have wellness and beauty centres: you can emerge detoxified, mentally alert and looking your best.

There are about 1300 thermal springs in Hungary, and some 300 of them are used for bathing – around 130 are in Budapest. There's so much thermal water that it is used to heat houses, but it doesn't do much for the plumbing. Steam baths can be traced back to Roman times and the Ottomans established Turkish baths, some of which are still in use today. Massage was important both then and now, and numerous different types of massage are available today.

While the spas all offer mineral waters, there is also medicinal water, which has proven medical benefits. Such water may ease aching joints, pain resulting from injuries, neuralgia, gout and rheumatism, but it may also be efficacious in helping people with skin conditions and gynaecological disorders. There are waters for bathing in and waters for drinking, which can be useful for alleviating digestive disorders and metabolic conditions. The relaxing treatments certainly relieve stress.

The health centres are carefully regulated. In 2003, the Ministry of Economy and Transport published a decree on wellness hotels, laying down requirements to be observed, and the National Tourist Office (see page 131) can provide information on approved centres and treatments. Doctors and trained assistants oversee treatments, as some techniques are contraindicated for patients with certain ailments, and medical approval is necessary to ensure that the bathing will be beneficial.

In Budapest, you have a choice: there are fitness and wellness hotels, or you can just visit the traditional baths and avail yourself of their services. Of the baths, the Gellért and the Széchenyi (see pages 39 and 70) are the grandest of them all, Art Nouveau and neo-Baroque palaces, respectively, with splendid baths and outdoor swimming pools. You can swim or have a mud-based body treat-

Hungary is famed for its baths

ment, massage or an underwater traction bath. The Gellért spa boasts an extensive menu of therapeutic services at the medicinal bath, though it specializes in rheumatology and pulmonology.

The Széchenyi Spa, one of Europe's largest bathing complexes, is located in Városliget (City Park). It also offers physiotherapy sessions and has a rheumatology department. The adventure pool is fitted with a water chute, underwater aeration, neck massage and water-jet massage points.

The sixteenth-century Rudas baths offer a taste of the Turkish art of bathing. Sunlight filters through holes carved into the domed ceilings, and stone arches ring the octagonal pools.

Taking the cure

Aside from spa waters, there are also cave cures, in which clean air and high humidity aid respiratory conditions; and there are dry baths using carbon dioxide of volcanic origin to improve heart and circulatory conditions and skin complaints.

SPORTS

Bowling: There are bowling alleys at the Mammut shopping centre (www.mammut.hu, www.bowlingclub.hu), as well as at some hotels.

Cycling: Budapest has nearly 200km (124 miles) of cycle paths. You can pick up the *Budapest for Bikers* map at tourist offices (see page 131). There's a public bike-sharing system called MOL BuBi, which costs HUF 120 to sign up and includes three minutes of bicycle usage, after which it costs HUF 40 per minute of use. There are 173 stations where bikes can be rented and returned. You can register with your bank card through the free MOL Bubi app (www.molbubi.hu).

Golf: Golfing greens are becoming popular in Hungary. The Hungarian Golf Federation (www.hungolf.hu) provides all the necessary information. There are also driving ranges around the capital. Further afield, there is an 18-hole course at the northern end of the long, narrow Szentendre Island opposite Visegrád, about 35 km (22 miles) from Budapest.

Tennis: More than 100 tennis courts are located at hotels, hostels and campsites. They charge around HUF 1,000 an hour. Detailed information is available from the Hungarian Tennis Association (Magyar Tenisz Szövetség; tel: 460-6807; www.huntennis.hu). Badminton and squash are also played.

Watersports: Windsurfing and yachting are possible on Lake Balaton, and boards and boats can be hired at the main resorts. Motorboats, however, are prohibited.

SPECTATOR SPORTS

The largest stadium in Budapest (and, indeed, in Hungary) is the Puskás Aréna (www.puskasarena.com), named after Hungarian footballing legend Ferenc Puskás. The stadium, which has a capacity of over 67,000, opened in 2019 on the site of the old Puskás Ferenc Stadion, demolished to make way for its modern successor. Close by is the Budapest Sportaréna (www.budapestarena.hu). As well as sporting events, the latter also hosts pop concerts. The nearest Metro is Puskás Ferenc Stadion.

Football: Football is Hungary's biggest spectator sport. Two of the most popular of Budapest's first-division teams are Budapest-Honvéd (who play at the newly opened Bozsik Aréna; www. honvedfc.hu) and Ferencváros (Groupama Aréna; www.fradi.hu).

Grand Prix: The annual Formula 1 Grand Prix meeting is held at the Hungaroring, about 19km (12 miles) east of Budapest.

SHOPPING

Budapest is no longer the bargain retail experience it once was, and prices for many goods are about the same as those in other European capitals. Shopping has undergone a revolution in Budapest in recent decades, a major development being the proliferation of shopping centres.

The largest is **Arena Mall** (Kerepesi út 9; www.arenamall.hu; close to Keleti railway station). Other large shopping complexes include the **Pólus Centre** (reached by bus from Keleti pu; www. polus-center.hu) and the **Westend City Centre** (Váci út 1–3; www.westend.hu), next to Nyugati railway station. **Mammut** and

Mammut II (www.mammut.hu) at Széll Kálmán tér are great favourites with local residents. On the other side of town, **Árkád** (www.arkadbudapest.hu) is a pleasant shopping centre located opposite the Örs Vezér tere metro terminal.

Budapest boutique

The retail centres are home to branches of many of the same chain stores that you find in other countries in Europe, including C&A, H&M, United Colors of Benetton, Virgin Megastore, Esprit, Mango, and Mexx, as well as some local chains. The other major change in shopping patterns has been the arrival in great force of super- and hypermarkets. Tesco, Interspar and Auchan are the leading supermarket chains in Hungary.

WHAT TO BUY

Visitors' shopping expeditions often start on **Váci utca**, a pedestrianized boulevard with a wide selection of shops; at its southern end, **Central Market Hall** (Vásárcsarnok) has an impressive array of high-quality food, as well as a cluster of craft stalls on its mezzanine level.

Ceramics and porcelain: Hungary is celebrated for its ceramics and porcelain. The **Herend** factory has been producing fine porcelain since 1826 and has a shop at Andrássy út 16 (www.herend.com). **Zsolnay** porcelain is also world-famous. The Budapest showroom is located at Rákóczi út 4–6 (www.zsolnay.hu).

Traditional-style plates and vases come in distinctive blue and white; there are ochre and floral-decorated glazed water jars from Mezőtúr, and local charcoal-coloured items, called 'black pottery'.

Chess sets: You will find beautiful sets with pawns in the guise of foot soldiers, and knights as hussars in eighteenth-century garb.

Woodwork: There is an abundance of children's toys, including puzzles and mobiles, made from wood, just like in the good old days. Boxes, bowls, walking sticks and other such items are also available. Holló Folkart Gallery (Vitkovics Mihály utca 12) is a good place to start.

Food and drink: Popular souvenirs include paprika in gift boxes or sachets; dried mushrooms, such as ceps and chanterelles; strudels packed in sturdy cardboard boxes; salami and goose-liver paté; and Hungarian wines (particularly Tokaj) and liqueurs, such as apricot brandy. The Budapest Wine Society (www.bortarsasag. hu) is a perfect place to go wine shopping. There are currently 16 shops in Budapest proper, and a further nine scattered throughout the surrounding countryside (a full list is available on the website).

HUNGARIAN EMBROIDERY

The oldest example of Hungarian embroidery is Stephen I's gold silk robe, now in the Hungarian National Museum (see page 55). Embroidery became a profession in medieval times and by the sixteenth century a style called úrihímzés was practised, the designs emanating from Renaissance Italy and Turkey. Hand-embroidered items can be bought at Folkart shops and at stalls. Look for intricate Halas lace, Matyó costumes, red-and-blue Palóc work (on aprons, towels and kerchiefs), and Kalocsa folk costumes. Prices can be high, as a great deal of handiwork is involved.

ENTERTAINMENT

Tickets for theatre, opera, ballet and classical concerts are more reasonably priced in Budapest than in many other cities, perhaps because
Hungarians don't generally see the arts as highbrow and elitist.

OPERA, CLASSICAL MUSIC AND BALLET

The newly renovated **Hungarian State Opera House** on Andrássy
út 22 is the finest of the city's opera venues and connoisseurs rank
it among Europe's best. Tickets are available at the box office (www.
opera.hu; email: ticket@boxoffice.hu). You can also purchase tickets online at www.jegymester.hu. Just around the corner from the
Opera, on Budapest's 'Broadway', is the Budapest Operetta Theatre
(Budapesti Operettszínház; Nagymező utca 17; tel: 312-4866; www.
operett.hu) which stages light opera and musicals – internationally
known ones as well as those written and produced in Hungary.

The Hungarian State Opera House, one of the best in Europe

Opera and ballet are also performed at the **Erkel Theatre** (Erkel Színház; II. János Pál pápa tér 30; www.opera.hu).

The city has a clutch of other fine halls *(színház)* for symphonies, concerts and opera, including the **Liszt Academy of Music** (Zeneakadémia; Liszt Ferenc tér 8; tel: 462-4600; www.zeneaka demia.hu), a splendid Art Nouveau music hall built in 1904, and **Pesti Vigadó** (Vigadó tér 1; www.vigado.hu). The **Bartók Béla Memorial House** (Bartók Béla Emlékház; Csalán út 29; www. bartokemlekhaz.hu; tel: 394-2100) has an intimate concert venue (with Bartók's own pianos); the Bartók String Quartet also sometimes gives concerts here. **St Stephen's Basilica**, the **Houses of Parliament**, the **Hilton Hotel** and the **Castle** are also used as venues. In summer, concerts are held in various parks and gardens, and there are even performances on boats and in cafés.

Budapest has music for all tastes. The **Budapest Congress Centre** (Budapesti Kongressusi Központ; tel: 372-5400; www.bcc.

hu) has a modern auditorium and moonlights as a music venue. It hosts many of the biggest names on the international classical music circuit.

Finally, there is the **Palace of Arts** complex (Művészetek Palotája; Komor Marcell utca 1; tel: 555-3000; www.mupa.hu), which contains the Béla Bartók Concert Hall (as well as the Ludwig Museum of Contemporary Art, the Festival Theatre and various other cultural hubs). Some of the smaller halls in the complex host children's concerts, jazz and world music performances.

THEATRE

The **National Theatre** (Nemzeti Színház; Bajor Gizi Park 1; tel: 476-6800; www.nemzetiszinhaz.hu) presents classic theatre, mostly in Hungarian. One of the best renowned dramatic theatres in Budapest is **Katona József Színház** (Petőfi Sándor utca 6; www.katonajozsefszinhaz.hu). The **Thália Theatre** (Nagymező utca 22–4; tel: 331-0635; www.thalia.hu) offers a varied popular programme. For contemporary dance drama with an alternative twist, visit **Trafó** (Liliom utca 41; tel: 456-2040; www.trafo.hu).

POP, ROCK AND JAZZ

Live music (including pop, rock, jazz and indie music), concert, festival and theatre tickets can be bought online at www.jegymester.hu. The city's biggest attraction for music fans is the week-long Sziget Festival (www.sziget.hu), which takes place in August each year and is one of the largest cultural and rock festivals in Europe with over 1000 performances.

TRADITIONAL MUSIC AND DANCE

Budapest is noted for *klezmer*, which is based on traditional Jewish music improvised by informal groups of musicians, and *táncház*, an urban revival of traditional rural Magyar dance. Called a 'dance-house movement', the latter arose as an expression of protest and national pride during communist rule in the 1970s and has produced some of the biggest names in Hungarian folk music. The centre for contemporary, world, gypsy, jazz and folk music is the **Fonó Music Club** (Sztregova utca 3; tel: 206-5300; www.fono. hu). *Táncház* is mostly performed during the winter months, but there are also summer festivals; see www.tanchaz.hu for information. Two other clubs to try are: **Kalamajka Táncház**, located at Aranytíz Cultural Centrum (Arany János utca 10, tel: 354-3400), and **Csángó Dance House** (Marczibányi tér 5/a) situated near the Széll Kálmán tér metro.

Look out, too, for the well-known professional group, **Muzsikás** (www.muzsikas.hu), which featured in the soundtrack for the film *The English Patient* (1996). They make occasional appearances in Budapest, especially during the Spring Festival (Budapesti Tavaszi Fesztivál; www.budapestitavaszifesztival.hu).

You can see Hungarian dancers, both emerging and established, most nights at the Municipal Folklore Center, Fehérvári út 47, south of Gellért Hill. The **Hungarian State Folklore Ensemble**, the **Danube Folklore Ensemble** and the **Rajkó Folk Ensemble** are all excellent performers. You can often catch them playing at the Budai Vigadó (Corvin tér 8) and Duna Palota (Zrinyi utca 5); see www.hungariakoncert.hu.

CLUBS AND BARS

Look for the sign *söröző* if you are a beer drinker, and *borozó* if you prefer wine. While a *söröző* is often similar to a German *Bierstube*, a *borozó* is rarely like a Parisian wine bar. Neither serve exclusively beer or wine.

The **Faust Wine Cellar**, tucked beneath Castle Hill, offers tasting sessions of all Hungary's speciality wines (www.gbwine.eu; Mon 2–5pm, Thurs 5–8pm, Fri–Sun 2–8pm).

Budapest has a lively nightlife

Beer-lovers will enjoy the **Belgian Brasserie Henri** (Bem rakpart 12; www.belgasorozo.com; daily noon–midnight) where you can wash down plates of *moules frites* with pints of Belgian beer.

If you'd like to become more closely acquainted with Hungarian beer, **Dreher** brewery have a beer museum – **Dreher sörmúzeum** (Jászberényi utca 7–11; Mon–Thurs 9am–4pm, Fri and Sat 9am–2pm; www.dreherzrt.hu).

Budapest also has a thriving club scene, with venues ranging from the chic to the shabby. Not to be missed are the ruin bars for which the city is famous: attracting a young, international crowd, the drinking dens are an eclectic blend of hip bar-pub-club-event space set in abandoned buildings and often decked out with street art, plants and vintage furniture. One of the coolest and best-established party spots in Budapest is the first ruin bar, **Szimpla Kert** (www.szimpla.hu), established in 2002 and set across two floors with a courtyard. There's always something happening here;

there is a party every night of the week, often with live music, and sometimes food or craft markets on Sundays. Other great drinking dens to check out include Csendes for a mellow night out and Mazel Tov for a slightly more upscale vibe.

CHILDREN'S BUDAPEST

There are lots of things for families to do in Budapest. First stop, in fine weather, could be to hire a family-sized pedal car in City Park or on Margaret Island. At Vajdahunyad Castle, there's summer boating and winter skating on the lake. Nearby is the Zoo and Holnemvolt Park, home to a splendid fun-fair (see page 69). There's a play area beside the **Feneketlen tó** (Bottomless Lake), which is home to ducks, fish, ringed snakes and tortoises. The Rail Heritage Park, Children's Railway and chairlift in the Buda Hills are also all popular (see pages 71, 76 and 45).

If the weather is bad, head for the **Campona Shopping Centre** (Nagytétényi út 37–45; bus from Gellért tér; www.campona. hu) for its Tropicarium, with fish, insects, snakes, birds and small mammals (www.tropicarium.hu), and the **Palace of Wonders** (Csodák Palotája; www.csopa.hu; daily 10am–7pm), an interactive scientific playhouse full of games and experiments. The **Natural History Museum** (Ludovika tér 2–6; www.nhmus.hu; daily 9am–5pm) offers hands-on exhibitions, while the **Puppet Theatre** (Bábszinház; Andrássy út 69; www.budapestbabszinhaz.hu) has daily performances for children.

There's an ice-rink (Jégpálya) at the **Pólus Shopping Centre** (Szentmihályi út 131); and rollerblades and skateboards are provided at **Görzenál Skatepark** (Árpád fejedelem utca; www. gorzenal.hu). At the **Orczy Kalandpark** (Orczy út 1; www.orczyka landpark.eu; March–Oct Sat and Sun 10am–6pm) children can enjoy canopy walks, ziplining and climbing.

WHAT'S ON

Dates of events and festivals can be obtained from Tourinform and IBUSZ offices. You can also check a calendar of events online on www.budapest bylocals.com orwww.budapestinfo.hu.

January/February. New Year's concerts. Farsang: carnival celebrations, street parades and parties.

March. National day (15th). Budapest Spring Festival: two weeks of performances by the best names in Hungarian music, theatre, dance, art and culture.

April. Cherry blossom festival at Fűvészkert Botanical Gardens.

May. May Day celebrations with varied programme, including concerts. Jazz Spring.

June. Budapest Summer Festival: open-air cinemas begin their screenings, and theatres stage light drama, musicals, opera, operetta and revues; shows on Margaret Island and in Városmajor Park. Danube Carnival – International Multicultural Festival: events with folk dance and music.

July. Budapest Pride, a week-long LGBTQ+ festival of events, culminating in a Pride march. Summer concert season continues.

August. Sziget Festival on Óbuda Island: one of the biggest rock and pop festivals in Europe. St Stephen's Day (20th), processions, Craftsmen's Fair in the Castle District, and firework display on Gellért Hill. Hungarian Grand Prix: Formula 1 cars race at the Hungaroring circuit. Jewish Summer Festival (end of August/beginning of September): music and art with Jewish themes.

September. Újbuda Jazz Festival. Budapest International Wine Festival: wine-tasting stalls at Vörösmarty tér, along with festivities and a street parade. International Book Festival (end of September/beginning of October): a celebration of literarure for keen readers.

October. Art Market: an international art fair, with renowned participants from all over the world. Revolution of 1956 Day (23rd).

November–December. Budapest Christmas Market at Vörösmarty tér. Christmas Fair by the Basilica.

FOOD AND DRINK

Magyar cuisine has a long history, but is little known outside Hungary. Traditionally, the nomadic Magyars cooked their food in a cauldron over an open fire, and traces of this kind of one-pot cooking can still be found in the hearty soups and cabbage-based dishes that crop up on many menus today. In the seventeenth century, paprika arrived in the country; some say the Slavs or the Turks brought it, others say it came from the Americas. Paprika is a relatively mild seasoning, which should not be confused with the far hotter chilli.

Hungarian food may be cooked in lard or goose fat, giving a heavier consistency and a richer taste than many Westerners are accustomed to. If restaurant portions are too hefty for you, order soup and then an appetizer instead of a main course. Some restaurants can offer smaller portions for light eaters.

Budapest has not always been noted for adventurous cooking, but things have changed recently. There is a new generation of chefs working in the city today that specializes in different culinary styles and has given an innovative twist to traditional dishes, breathing new life into age-old recipes.

Paprika, Hungary's 'red gold'

Inside Costes, a Michelin-starred restaurant

Where to eat

You won't often see the sign 'restaurant' in Budapest; when you do, the establishment is likely to cater to foreign tourists. The two most common names for a place to eat are *étterem* and *vendéglő*. A *csárda* (pronounced *chard-a*) is usually a country-style inn with a cosy atmosphere. Budapest has long rivalled Vienna for its café culture and love of pastries and coffee. Many cafés (*kávéház* and *cukrászda*) serve full meals as well as cakes.

When to eat

Breakfast (*reggeli*) is generally served 7–10am. Hungarians don't eat much at the start of the day, but at most hotels a basic international breakfast buffet is served. Lunch (*ebéd*), generally dished up 1–3pm, is the main meal of the day, a fact reflected in the quantities that tend to be served. Dinner (*vacsora*) is usually 7–10pm, though Hungarians in general are not late eaters.

What to eat

Starters (*előételek*): Goose-liver paté and *hideg libamáj*, cold slices of goose liver served in its own fat on toast with purple onion, are Hungarian favourites (the latter is also served as a main course). Pancakes (*palacsinta*) Hortobágy-style are filled with minced meat, deep-fried until crispy, and topped with sour cream. Budapest is also a good place to try caviar (*kaviár*). The best is often Caspian.

Soups (*leves*): Soups are immensely popular and always on the menu. The well-known *gulyásleves* (goulash soup) is the standard bearer: chunks of beef, potatoes, onions, tomatoes and peppers are cooked with paprika, garlic and caraway for a burst of flavour. Fishermen's soup (*halászlé*) is also based on potatoes, onions, tomatoes and paprika, with the addition of chunks of freshwater fish. Also popular – and actually a meal in itself – is *babgulyás*, goulash soup served with dried beans. If you prefer a lighter soup, try consommé with quail eggs (*eroleves fürjtojással*). You're also likely to find garlic cream soup served in a hollowed-out loaf.

Perhaps the most intriguing of all is *hideg meggyleves* (cold sour-cherry soup). Topped with frothy whipped cream, it would certainly be classified as a dessert elsewhere. On a hot day, try *hideg almaleves* – a creamy, refreshing cold apple soup, dusted with cinnamon.

Full-fat snacks

Hungarians love *lángos*, which is deep-fried batter, made more enticing by slathering it with garlic, cheese and sour cream. There are stands serving *lángos* at markets across the city.

Meat (*húsételek*): Hungary is a nation of carnivores. Pörkölt is the stew that most closely approximates the West's notion of goulash. It can be made with beef, chicken or pork. *Maharpörkölt* is beef stew and *borjúpörkölt* is veal stew; the list is as long as the meats available. Veal

Töltött káposzta is a speciality

and pork are the top choice of most Hungarians, whether fried, stewed or stuffed with combinations of ham, cheese, mushrooms or asparagus. Steaks, too, are usually on the menu. *Lecsó* is a stew of peppers, tomatoes and onions. *Töltött káposzta* is another classic: cabbage leaves wrapped around pork and rice, served over sauerkraut with spicy sausage, paprika and a generous dollop of sour cream.

Game and fowl: Game is a stalwart on dining tables across Hungary. Wild boar (*vaddisznó*) and venison (*oz*) frequently appear on restaurant menus, often reasonably priced. Chicken (*csirke*) is popular and inexpensive, and *csirke-paprikás* – chicken stewed with onions, green peppers, tomatoes, sour cream and paprika – ranks as something of a national dish. Goose is another favourite, prized for its flesh as well as its liver. Turkey often comes stewed or in stuffed portions, Kyiv-style (with garlic butter) or with ham and cheese. Look out, too, for stag, hare, pheasant and wild duck.

Fish (*halételek*): Local fish in this land-locked country is necessarily of the freshwater variety; *ponty* (carp) and *fogas* (pike-perch from Lake Balaton) are the two most commonly found in Budapest, but they are somewhat bland. A tasty fish soup, served with paprika, is *halászlé*.

Vegetables and pasta: Vegan and vegetarian restaurants can be found across the city, and meat-free dishes are increasingly cropping up on Hungarian menus. Vegetable accompaniments sometimes have to be ordered separately and can be uninspired. In some establishments, you can get a fine Caesar or Greek salad but in others *saláta* may be little more than a plate of cabbage and pickled beetroot. What most Westerners call a mixed salad usually appears as *vitamin saláta*. Strict vegetarians will need to monitor the menu closely: classic dishes of stuffed pepper (*töltött paprika*) and stuffed cabbage (*töltött káposzta*) include pork in the filling, and many vegetable soups are cooked with meat or meat stock.

Dishes are usually served with boiled potatoes or with pasta, either in ribbon noodles (*nokedli*) or in the form of starchy dumplings (*galuska*), often translated as gnocchi on the menu.

Desserts (*tészták*): Hungarians love pastries and sweets, and two desserts are ubiquitous. One is the decadent Gundel pancake (*Gundel palacsinta*), named after Hungary's most famous restaurateur. It is filled with nut and raisin paste, drenched in chocolate and rum sauce, and sometimes flambéed. The equally calorific *somlói galuska* is a heavy sponge with vanilla, nuts, chocolate and whipped cream in an orange and rum sauce. Strudels (*rétes*) often have fruit and poppy-seed fillings. For simpler tastes, there is ice cream (*fagylalt*), cheese (*sajt*) or fruit (*gyümölcs*).

Drinks

Hungarian wines: The Great Plain, in southern Hungary, produces a wide range of wines, from vigorous and full-bodied reds to dry, smoky whites. The most famous of the white wines is Tokay (Tokaj), a rich, aged dessert wine. The grapes behind this world-renowned wine are grown in the volcanic soil of the Tokay region in the northeast of Hungary. The fruit is left on the vine until autumn mists encourage the growth of the noble rot that gives the wine its intense sweetness and complex character. Tokay has a rich viticultural history dating over 200 years, and was a favourite of Catherine the Great and Louis XIV; it also inspired poetry from Voltaire and music from Schubert. Tokaji Furmint is dry, Tokaji Szamorodni is medium-sweet, akin to sherry, and Tokaji Aszú is full-bodied and sweet.

Less celebrated but perfectly satisfying white table wines come from the Lake Balaton region, including Riesling, Sauvignon Blanc and Chardonnay. Badacsonyi wines are the best known and have been enjoyed in Hungary for around 2000 years. Some of the best white wines in the country come from the smallest wine-producing region, Somló.

The Villány region churns out some of Hungary's finest reds, many of which are aged in oak casks, including the fine Villányi Burgundi and the tannic Kékoportó. The best-known Hungarian red, which comes from the northeastern region, is the splendidly named Egri Bikavér (Bull's Blood of Eger) – a full-bodied and spicy

Wine is a staple in Hungary

accompaniment to meat or game dishes. More subtle is the Pinot Noir from the same town.

Beer (sör): Hungarian beers go well with heavy, spicy foods. Except at the most formal restaurants, beer is as acceptable as wine to accompany a meal.

Other drinks: There are no recognized Hungarian apéritifs, but a Puszta cocktail – a punchy concoction of apricot brandy, local cognac-style brandy, and sweet Tokay wine – is as good a way as any to start the evening.

Finish off your evening with one of Hungary's famous fruit brandies (*pálinka*). They are fermented from the fruit and therefore have a clean, dry taste. The favourite is *barack* (apricot), followed by *cseresznye* (cherry). The country's national drink, the curious green herbal liqueur called Zwack Unicum, has been knocked back for centuries.

Coffee (kávé): This is a favourite Budapest drink, commonly served black, hot and sweet, espresso-style in thimble-sized cups. There used to be no alternative but now you'll find milk available everywhere and cappuccinos on offer in Budapest and other large towns. Tea is also widely available in decent coffeehouses.

CLINKING GLASSES

It's probably better not to clink glasses when drinking a toast. It is said that in 1849, when the Austrians executed 13 Hungarian revolutionaries, they were drinking, cheering and clinking glasses between each execution. Since then, many Hungarians have felt that it was insensitive to continue this tradition. However, as the year 1999 approached, there were stories that the 'curse' was to run for only 150 years and then cease, so glasses may now be clinked in toasts. To avoid mistakes, its best to take your lead from the company you're in.

TO HELP YOU ORDER
Waiter **Pincér**
Menu **Étlap**
Enjoy your meal. **Jó étvágyat.**
The bill, please. **Kérem a számlát.**
I'd like (an/some)… **Kérek szépen…**

MENU READER

alma apple
ásvány víz mineral water
bab beans
bárány lamb
borjú veal
csípos hot (spicy)
csirke chicken
fehér bor white wine
fogas pike-perch
fózött boiled
gomba mushroom
gulyás goulash
gyümölc fruit
hagyma onion
halak fish
halászlé fish stew
húsételek meat dishes
kacsa duck
káposzta cabbage
kávé coffee
kenyér bread
leves(ek) soup

liba goose
marha beef
paradiscom tomato
pisztráng trout
ponty carp
pörkölt stew
ránsott sajt fried cheese
sajt cheese
saláták salad
sertés pork
sör beer
sútve baked/fried
tea tea
tej milk
tészta pasta
tonhal tuna
vad game
vajat butter
víz water
vörös bor red wine
zöldság vegetables

WHERE TO EAT

We have used the following symbols to give an idea of the price for a three-course meal for one, including wine, cover and service:

€€€€	**over 60 euros**
€€€	**30–60 euros**
€€	**20–30 euros**
€	**below 20 euros**

BUDA AND ÓBUDA

21 Magyar Vendéglő €€€ *I Fortuna utca 21, tel: 202-2113,* www.21restaurant.hu. A relative newcomer to the Castle District, this restaurant is raising the culinary bar by serving decent dishes at a fair price. The style of food is solid Central European fare: expect the likes of *Wiener schnitzel*, roast duckling and pike perch.

Aranyszarvas €€€ *I Szarvas tér 1,* www.aranyszarvasetterem.hu. Occupying the historic *Golden Stag Inn* at the foot of Castle Hill near the Medical History Museum, this restaurant is not short on atmosphere or character. The food is well prepared – Hungarian with a French twist – and the wine list offers a good opportunity to sample some of Hungary's finest bottles. There is a picturesque terrace for outdoor dining in the summer months.

Hemingway €€€ *XI Kosztolányi Dezső tér 2, tel: 488-6000,* www.hemingway-etterem.hu. The proprietor is an Ernest Hemingway fan, and the decor evokes the writer's world. The menu is seasonal and includes, of course, swordfish. There's a large choice of teas, coffees and cigars on offer, too. The restaurant is located by Fenekentlen tó (meaning bottomless lake) in a pleasant park near Móricz Zsigmond Körtér.

Kéhli Vendéglő €€€ *III Mókus utca 22, tel: 368-0613,* www.kehli.hu. *Kéhli* is a family-owned local tavern that was once the haunt of author Gyula Krúdy (1877–1933). The marrow-bone hotpot relished by Krúdy is still on the menu, which also offers Hungarian and international cuisine. Top your meal with a Hungarian Trifle (*somlói galuska*).

KicsiZso € *II, Frankel Leó utca 11*. Cosy breakfast joint at the Buda end of Margít híd, where you squeeze past the locals to reach your table. Ham and eggs, baguettes, and a daily lunch menu. Breakfast is available all day – the coffee is excellent. Weather permitting, you can sit at the long table outside.

Marxim € *II Kisrókus utca 23, tel: 316-0231*, www.marxim.hu. Appropriately – given its name – this popular little place is located near Széll Kálmán tér. Workers of the world unite for pizza served with panache. The menu shows considerable black humour, although *Gulagpizza* is said to be more nourishing than it sounds. The decor is propaganda of the past, the music is loud and the opening hours are long (until 1am Sun–Thurs and until 2am Fri and Sat).

Nagyi Palacsintázója € *I Batthyány tér 5*. A popular fast-food crêpe restaurant, with several branches scattered across the city (this one has decent views over the Parliament), packed with locals and tourists alike. If you don't have a sweet tooth, choose from the wide selection of savoury crêpes – ham and cheese, mushroom, spinach, broccoli-chicken or cottage cheese. Delicious, good value for money and open round the clock.

Náncsi Néni Vendéglője €€€ *II Ördögárok utca 80, tel: 397-2742*, www.nancsineni.hu. A traditional restaurant, with garlic and paprika dangling from the ceiling and gingham cloths and fresh bread on the tables. Pickles on the shelves can be purchased. There's a garden, so it is often thrumming with families. Auntie Neni's home cooking is traditional, rustic Hungarian fare and it is served in heaped helpings. The restaurant is located in the Buda Hills, near the Hüvösvölgy terminal of the Children's Railway.

Röma Ételbár € *I Csalogány utca 20, tel: 190-7773*. This is how restaurants used to be in Budapest – ramshackle, noisy and full of the smell of paprika-spiked cooking. It offers lunchtime service only, and satiates local office-workers with paprika mushrooms, home-made noodles, pork ribs fried in breadcrumbs and pancakes.

Ruszwurm Cukrászda €€€ I *Szentháromság utca 7, tel: 375-5284*, www.ruszwurm.hu. Established in 1827, *Ruszwurm* is the oldest confectionary in Buda. Located in the vicinity of the Matthias Church, it's the perfect place to take a break and treat yourself to the chocolate Ruszwurm torta in the cosy Biedermeyer-stye interior.

PEST

Bagolyvár Étterem €€€ *XIV Gundel Károly út 4*, www.bagolyvar.com. The *Bagolyvár Étterem*, located just off Heroes' Square, offers a budget-friendly alternative to its sister restaurant, *Gundel*, just round the corner. The ambience is more informal, and the food more rustic, but the tastiness of the Hungarian cuisine is no less pleasing.

Borkonyha Winekitchen €€€ *V Sas utca 3, tel: 266-0835*, www.borkonyha.hu. A Michelin-starred, wine-oriented restaurant situated right in the heart of Pest. It offers the best of traditional Hungarian cuisine with a contemporary touch. The name *Winekitchen* speaks for itself – the wine list is extensive and diverse, but most of them are Hungarian; 48 out of 200 wines are offered by the glass.

Café Kör €€ *V Sas utca 17, tel: 311-0053*, www.facebook.com/cafekor restaurant. Situated near Deák Ferenc tér, *Café Kör* is a warm and welcoming spot with crisp white tablecloths, friendly service and reasonable prices. It is popular with locals and tourists alike, and you will need to book ahead for peak times. Goose-liver paté, spit roast, mixed grill, duck and some fine puddings ensure return visits. Small portions can be ordered for about 70 percent of full price.

Centrál Kávéház €€ *V Károlyi Mihály utca 9*, www.centralkavehaz.hu. This legendary café first opened in 1887 and reopened in 2000 after nearly a half century's dormancy. Famous Hungarian artists and writers used to frequent it; now it's a useful option for a good, affordable meal at any time of day. The menu includes soups, salads, sandwiches and more elaborate meals, as well as a wide selection of cakes and pies. The house speciality, *Pesti Kávé*, literally a strong 'coffee from Pest', garnished with whipped cream and served with a blueberry-jam macaroon, is well worth a try.

Costes €€€€ *IX Ráday utca 4,* www.costes.hu. Chef Eszter Pallagyi presents refined dishes inspired by culinary influences from around the world, without losing sight of the robust flavours and traditions of Hungarian cuisine. Alongside meat and fish showpieces, there are season-driven dishes on the menu. Diners at this Michelin-starred restaurant can choose between a four-, five-, six-, or seven-course menu. In 2015, the sister restaurant *Costes Downtown* opened in Vigyázó Ferenc Street 5; just a year later, it too was awarded a Michelin star.

Cyrano €€€ *V Kristóf tér 7–8, tel: 266-3096,* www.cyrano.hu. This chic restaurant is located right in the centre of town near Váci utca. The menu is French/Mediterranean-leaning but with traditional Hungarian touches. Inside, the ostentatious decor features the chandelier from the film set of *Cyrano De Bergerac*, starring Gérard Depardieu.

Fatál €€ *V Váci utca 67, tel: 266-2607,* www.fatalrestaurant.com. The exterior offers little clue as to what *Fatál* might offer and the name sounds a bit dubious, but it means 'wooden platter' in Hungarian, and the sharing plates come heaped with Hungarian food, mostly meaty. The clientele are mainly tourists, but the food is good and the prices reasonable for Váci utca.

Félix Hélix € *VII, Kazinczy utca 52/b*. It's easy to miss this dinky bar, located on the walk between Kazinczy utca and Holló utca, as it's an unassuming haunt that doesn't shout about itself. That's partly the appeal of the place, squeezed between the brash bars in the middle of Seventh District partyland. The Irish-Egyptian duo behind it turn out a marvellous range of foods that you won't find anywhere else, such as cucumber soup with goat's milk and Moroccan-style beef with couscous. There is folk music of different kinds on Thursdays, and you'll find backgammon boards up in the gallery.

Fészek Klub €€ *VII Kertész utca 36, tel: 342-6549,* www.feszek-muveszklub.hu. Tucked away in a charmingly dilapidated garden courtyard in the city's old artists' club, this restaurant serves genuine Hungarian home-cooking such as Reform *bárány* (roast lamb), ragout of wild boar and freshwater fish dishes.

Gerbeaud €€€ *V Vörösmarty tér 7–8,* www.gerbeaud.hu. Established in 1858, the café is legendary. Chandeliers, marble tables and lavish decor retain the spirit of a bygone age. *Gerbeaud* is renowned for cakes, including *Dobos torta* and *Esterházy torta*, as well as cappuccino but it is so much more than that. In 2007, it opened a haute-cuisine restaurant, *Onyx* (see page 112).

Gresham Restaurant €€€ *V Széchenyi István tér 5–6*, www.fourseasons.com. Sheltered within the elegant *Four Seasons Hotel Gresham Palace*, this fine restaurant has a glass frontage that frames views of the square, the Chain Bridge and the Danube. The style of cooking is Hungarian meets Italian, and talented chefs give high-quality produce the precise and balanced execution it deserves. The wine list is of high quality, the service pleasantly discreet.

Gundel €€€€ *XIV Gundel Károly út 4*, www.gundel.hu. Hungary's most famous restaurant, founded in 1894, *Gundel* is a byword for Hungarian haute cuisine, and remains the haunt of the elite. The Art Nouveau decor and atmosphere have been maintained but the menu is up to date, featuring international as well as Hungarian gourmet delights, such as *fogas* (pike-perch). Be sure to save room for the famous *palacsinta* – pancakes stuffed with rum, raisins, lemon rind and walnuts, served with chocolate sauce. It isn't cheap, but the set business lunches and the Sunday brunch are very reasonable. It's formal, so jackets are required for men, relatively smart dress for women, and you need to make a reservation.

Kashmir €€ *V Arany János utca 13*, www.kashmiretterem.hu. The owner of this restaurant, Allen Diwan, trained with Atul Kochhar, London's first Michelin-starred Indian chef, and as you might expect with this pedigree, the North Indian cuisine here is a cut above the average. The menu includes many vegetarian options, and the buffet lunch is a particular bargain.

Két Szerecsen €€€ *VI, Nagymező utca 14*, www.ketszerecsen.hu. Buzzy place nicely secreted away just off Andrássy út, which is good for coffee and break-fast or full-blown supper. The most appealing aspect, though, is the tapas menu (veggie, meat, seafood), which can be taken individually or as an assortment. A varied mains menu includes salmon steamed in white wine, and a Thai green curry. There's a lovely terrace in summer.

Kisharang Étkezde €€ *V Október 6 utca 17*, www.kisharang.hu. Lunchtimes are always bustling and convivial at this little restaurant just round the cor-

WHERE TO EAT 111

ner from the Basilica of St Stephen. Visitors will have to compete with hungry local office workers for homely meals of goose-dumpling soup, schnitzels, paprika chicken and pancakes.

Köleves Vendéglő €€ *VII Kazinczy utca 41*, www.kolevesvendeglo.hu. This bright and unpretentious restaurant in the Jewish Quarter offers classic Hungarian-Jewish cuisine as well as a range of excellent vegetarian dishes. A speciality on Fridays, Saturdays and Sundays is Jewish baked beans with smoked goose leg.

M €€€ *VII, Kertész utca 48*. This small boho-style bistro is just the spot for a low-key evening dalliance. The small menu changes daily and can throw up some surprises: rabbit kidneys. Standouts include duck breast with wild mushroom risotto, and shoulder of rabbit in garlic and thyme with ratatouille. Booking essential.

Mátyás Pince €€€ *V Március 15 tér 7*. The *Mátyás Pince* is one of Pest's most popular tourist spots, serving traditional Hungarian dishes in an atmospheric turn-of-the-century cellar setting. Anyone with a healthy appetite should try the King Mátyás Platter. To round off the tourist experience, there's traditional music as a soundtrack to your meal.

Menza €€ *VI Liszt Ferenc tér 2*, www.menzaetterem.hu. One of many bars and restaurants clustered around this square, *Menza*'s decor is an exercise in retro styling, recreating the look of a 1970s cafeteria but with comfort and a dash of urban chic. The young and lively clientele flock here for the extensive cocktail list as well as for the menu of updated Central European classics.

Montenegrói Gurman € *VII, Rákóczi út 54*, www.mnggurman.com. Fans of the traditional Balkan grill should make this place their first port of call. Gut-busting portions of succulent *čevapčići* (spiced mincemeat rissoles) and *pljeskavica* (hamburger-style patty) served with spicy paprika and *lepinja* (doughy bread), and all washed down with a bottle of Slovenian Laško beer. Just the job.

Okay Italia €€ *V Szent István körút 20, tel: 349-2991*, www.okayitalia.hu. This dependable and reasonably priced Italian restaurant gives you a night off from goulash and the other Hungarian staples. The pizza, pasta and risotto are popular with visitors and locals alike.

Onyx €€€€ *V Vörösmarty tér 7–8, tel: 30-508-0622,* www.onyxrestaurant.hu. *Onyx* is the brainchild of the talented team behind *Gerbeaud* and is located in the same block in the centre of town. This haute-cuisine restaurant offers precision cooking using high-quality ingredients, and has scooped a well-deserved Michelin star for its efforts. The decor is smart and chic, with starched white table-linen and lacquered furnishings.

Spinoza €€€ *VII, Dob utca 15,* www.spinozahaz.hu. In the heart of the old Jewish quarter, this popular restaurant has a very cultured feel – not least because the small theatre at the back has performances and readings every night. Don't miss the Jewish evening of music and food on Fridays. It has a big menu, including salads and sandwiches, alongside Hungarian favourites such as goose leg with red cabbage and potatoes, and the soft drinks menu is filled with interesting options like elderflower and lavender lemonades. Also offers a great lunch menu.

Tom-George Restaurant and Lounge €€€ *V Október 6 utca 8,* www. tomgeorge.hu. *Tom-George*, set near the Basilica of St Stephen, has a large design-conscious interior and caters mainly to a young and lively crowd. The extensive menu offers international and Italian food, with the occasional nod towards Hungarian cuisine. Considering the location, the prices are quite reasonable. The cocktail list is sizeable and makes this a good place for the first stop when planning a night on the town.

TRAVEL ESSENTIALS

PRACTICAL INFORMATION

A

ACCESSIBLE TRAVEL

Budapest is generally improving for travellers with disabilities and access needs. Currently, accessibility ranges from excellent to non-existent. Public transport is difficult for disabled passengers, but there are now buses equipped to take wheelchairs on some routes; trams and buses tend to be more accessible than the metro. The BKK mobile app, BKK Futár, has an accessible journey planner.

Furthermore, there is a door-to-door taxi-like service with special minibuses fitted with hydraulic lifts which can be called upon (BKK; www.bkv.hu; tel: 499-8340). A few metro stations now have lifts. Some museums are accessible. The spa hotels are fully equipped, and many larger hotels have some adapted rooms and wheelchair access.

ACCOMMODATION

As well as hotels (see page 133), visitors can stay in a *panzió* (pension/bed-and-breakfast hotel). Many of these are set on the fringes of the city, in the suburbs or the Buda Hills with the added advantage of serenity, greenery and great views. Self-catering apartments and rooms in private homes are a growing sector; Airbnb (www.airbnb.co.uk) is a popular site for finding this kind of accommodation.

Accommodation in private homes is well established in the Lake Balaton area, as the numerous German *Zimmer frei* (vacant room) signs indicate. Campsites are plentiful in Hungary, and there are eight in the environs of Budapest. It may come as a surprise, but many Hungarian hotels generally accept pets. See also Youth Hostels, page 132.

AIRPORT

The **Budapest Liszt Ferenc International Airport** (BUD; formerly Budapest Ferihegy; tel: 296-7000; www.bud.hu) is 38km (24 miles) east of the capital. Terminal 2A serves flights in the Schengen zone and Terminal 2B serves all non-Schengen destinations (until 2012, there used to be Terminal 1, hence the names 2A and 2B). Both terminals are connected by the Sky-Court, a state-of-the art passenger hall. The airport has the usual car-hire desks, bureaux de change, ATM machines and information offices, and wifi is available free of charge. There is an observation terrace at the Terminal 2A departure hall.

It takes about 45 minutes to get from the airport to the centre of Budapest. The efficient **Airport Minibus** (www.airportshuttle.hu; email info@hotelsshuttle.hu; WhatsApp: +36 7094 67901) is the best deal; it is a shared taxi that will deliver you to, and collect you from, any address in Budapest. Look for the prominent 'Airport Minibus' sign at the information desk. For the return journey, email or WhatsApp at least 24 hours in advance to book.

miniBUD Airport Shuttle Services (www.minibud.hu) take passengers to exact locations in the city centre from around 4,400 HUF per person and can be booked in advance. There is also a **public airport bus**: No. 200E (BKV; www.bkv.hu), which is much cheaper (one-way ticket is HUF 350, and HUF 450 when bought from the driver) and deposits passengers at the Kőbánya-Kispest metro station; and No. 100E, which is probably the most useful as it takes passengers to the city centre; a one-way ticket is HUF 2,200. You can check the 100E schedule online at www.bkk.hu/en/travel-information/public-transport/airport-shuttle.

If you want to take a **taxi**, there are plenty parked just outside the airport boundaries, waiting for radio calls from their offices. Once a call is received, the taxi will be with you in minutes. Avoid the touts looking for custom. The reputable companies are available at the terminal (Fő taxi, www.fotaxi.hu; Tele 5, www.tele5taxi.hu; 6x6 Taxi, www.6x6taxi.hu). Always clarify the rate before setting out. For example, a ride from the airport to the Castle district should cost approximately €22.

A final option is to use a rideshare app; Uber is banned in Budapest but similar companies such as **Bolt** work in much the same way; a trip from the airport to the city centre with Bolt will cost around HUG 7,000 and take about half an hour.

B

BUDAPEST CARD

The Budapest Card (Budapest Kártya; www.budapest-card.com) allows the holder 24, 48, 72, 96 or 120 hours of travel and sightseeing. A booklet comes with the card, detailing all the services available. These include free travel on public transport; free admission to museums and baths; free walking tours; and discounts at restaurants and shops and on tickets for cultural programmes and for many other attractions.

The Budapest Card costs €33 for 24 hours, €49 for 48 hours, €63 for 72 hours, €77 for 96 hours and €92 for 120 hours. It is available to buy online or at the airport, Budapest tourist information points, most hotels and main metro stations.

BUDGETING FOR YOUR TRIP

Visitors expecting the dirt-cheap Central Europe of the past may be in for a shock, as shops and many restaurants in Budapest charge the same prices as Western European countries.

One thing that does remain very inexpensive, however, is the highly efficient public-transport system.

Transport to Budapest. Since May 2004, when Hungary joined the European Union, a number of budget airlines have been running services from various European cities. Non-Europeans can expect their flights to eat up considerably more of their budgets.

Local transport. Public transport (see page 128) is very inexpensive. If you have to take a taxi, always phone for one or use the Bolt app rather than hailing a ride in the street.

Incidentals. Museum admission fees for adults range from HUF 500 to HUF 2000. Prices for entertainment are typically as follows: tickets for theatre, musicals and classical music concerts range from HUF 700 to HUF 5000, although much-anticipated performances at the Hungarian Opera House can cost up to HUF 10,000.

C

CAR HIRE

The minimum age requirement to hire a car is 21 years, and you must have been in possession of a valid licence for at least 12 months. It is best to book in advance.

Rates vary (upwards from HUF 30,000 for 3 days) for an economy-size car. Always ask if CDW (collision damage waiver) insurance is included in the price. The major agencies have offices at the airport and in Pest.

CLIMATE

Budapest is very cold in winter and sweltering in July and August. The best weather is from May to early June and September to October. Average day-time temperatures are as follows:

	J	F	M	A	M	J	J	A	S	O	N	D
°C	5	6	10	13	19	21	23	22	20	14	8	6
°F	41	43	50	55	66	70	74	72	68	57	46	41

CLOTHING

Dress is indistinguishable from that in any other European capital. Dress smartly in casinos and more upmarket restaurants.

CRIME AND SAFETY

Budapest has a low rate of violent crime, but as in all major cities, use common sense, don't take risks and be wary of pickpockets. Keep a close eye on your belongings, especially on the metro or in crowded places.

It's wise to make photocopies of travel documents and keep them in a separate place, such as locked securely a hotel safe. Theft should be reported to police at a police station, of which there are plenty in the city. Remember to get a copy of your statement for your own insurance purposes. The emergency services phone number is 112.

CUSTOMS AND ENTRY REQUIREMENTS

Most visitors require a valid passport to enter Hungary. Since joining the European Union, citizens of other EU countries require only an ID card. Citizens of many non-European countries do not need visas, either; visitors from the UK, for example, can visit Hungary without a visa for up to 90 days in any 180-day period, provided their passport is valid for at least three months after the day they plan to leave. The Ministry of Foreign Affairs maintains a helpful and up-to-the minute website reporting requirements and changes (www. konzuliszolgalat.kormany.hu). Those who need visas may obtain them from the Hungarian consulate in their country of residence. There are single, double- and multiple-entrance visas.

The Hungarian National Tax and Customs Administration (NTCA) also runs a website (www.nav.gov.hu) giving details of regulations. Travellers may bring 200 cigarettes, a litre of spirits and two litres of wine; no meat, dairy or perishable food is allowed from non-EU destinations. However, there are no restrictions to the amount of alcohol and cigarettes visitors travelling from another EU country may bring into Hungary, provided the goods are all for personal use, and not for sale. There have been no currency restrictions since 2000, although leaving or entering the EU with large amounts of cash – €10,000 or more – should be declared.

Value-added tax, or VAT (known as ÁFA in Hungary), can be reclaimed on goods costing more than HUF 50,000 (by non-EU residents only). Shops participating in the scheme are responsible for making the refund to travellers who are entitled to it.

D

DRIVING

To take your car into Hungary you need a valid driving licence and car registration papers. Cars from most European countries are presumed to be fully insured, so no extra documentation needs to be shown.

Road conditions. Hungary has one of the highest accident rates in Europe, and Budapest drivers are notorious for their recklessness. Central Budapest boulevards are many lanes wide, and you have to contend with trams and trolley buses as well as heavy traffic.

Hungary's expanding motorway system is well maintained and expanding. An e-vignette is required for most sections of Hungarian motorways. For a passenger car, these cost €176 for a year; €32 for a month; and €20 for 10 days. E-vignettes can be bought online at www.motorway.hu (National Toll Payment Services PLC; tel. 06-40/40-50-60 from Hungary, or +36-36/587-500 from abroad) or www.tolltickets.com, as well as at retailers such as service and petrol stations, and at the Hegyeshalom border crossing. Yellow emergency telephones are spaced every few kilometres along motorways M1, M5 and M7, and along the No 5 highway. Telephone 188 for help from the **Hungarian Automobile Club** anywhere in Hungary, day or night (Magyar Autóklub; www.autoklub.hu).

Rules and regulations. These are based on the Vienna and Geneva conventions, so general international regulations apply. Drive on the right and pass on the left, but be careful at all times. Cars must be fitted with a nationality plate or sticker. A set of spare bulbs, a first-aid kit and a warning triangle are also obligatory. Seatbelts are compulsory in front and back seats; children under 12 are prohibited from travelling in the front seat. Motorcycle riders and passengers must wear crash helmets. Using a hand-held mobile phone while driving is prohibited. Don't drink and drive: any amount of alcohol in the bloodstream is a punishable offence.

Speed limits. These are 130kmh (80mph) on motorways, 110kmh (68mph) on highways, 90kmh (55mph) on major roads, and 50kmh (31mph) in built-up areas, with on-the-spot fines for speeding. In resorts and built-up areas where there are lots of children, a 30kmh (18mph) speed limit may be imposed. Look for signs.

Fuel (_benzin_). Petrol stations are frequent along highways and main roads, but don't venture down minor roads without filling up. Stations are usually open 6am–10pm; there is 24-hour service in the populated areas. Unleaded fuel is widely available. You can usually pay for petrol with a credit card. If an attendant fills your car, you should give them a small tip.

Parking. There are meters, and public car parks. Try to find a hotel with a car park, leave your car there and take the metro. A car parked in a prohibited zone will be towed away or clamped.

If you need help. Remember to put out a red warning triangle 50 metres (165ft) behind your car. In the event of an accident, call the police (tel: 107) or the emergency number (tel: 112). This is compulsory if anyone is injured, and even if there are no injuries, there may be claims for damage or other consequences. If matters are serious, foreign citizens have a right to an interpreter and a lawyer. Cars with damaged bodywork are allowed out of the country only if they have an official certificate for the damage.

> Full tank, please. **Kérem, töltse tele a tankot.**
> I've broken down. **Meghibásodott a kocsim.**
> There's been an accident. **Baleset történt.**
> Can I park here? **Szabad itt parkolnom?**

E

ELECTRICITY

The current is 220 volts throughout Hungary. Take a two-pin adapter as necessary.

EMBASSIES AND CONSULATES

Australia: Enquires should be directed to the Australian embassy in Austria, Gertrude-Fröhlich-Sandner-Straße 2, Vienna; tel: +43-1-506740; www.austria. embassy.gov.au

Canada: Ganz utca 16; tel: 392-3360; www.canadainternational.gc.ca

Ireland: V Szabadság tér 7 (in Bank Centre); tel: 301-4960; www.dfa.ie/irish-embassy/hungary

South Africa: II Gárdonyi Géza út 17; tel: 392-0999

UK: Füge utca 5-7; tel: 266-2888; www.gov.uk/government/world/organisations/british-embassy-budapest

US: Szabadság tér 12; tel: 475-4400; https://hu.usembassy.gov

EMERGENCIES

Emergency telephone numbers throughout Hungary are as follows:

General Emergency **112**

Ambulance **104**

Fire **105**

Police **107**

English-speaking 24-hour medical service, tel: 200-0100

G

GETTING THERE

Air travel. EasyJet (www.easyjet.com), Eurowings (www.eurowings.com), Ryanair (www.ryanair.com), WizzAir (www.wizzair.com) and others fly to Budapest from various European cities. British Airways (www.britishairways.com), Lufthansa (www.lufthansa.com) and KLM (www.klm.com) also run flights to Budapest. There are plenty of options and low fares.

Rail travel. Budapest can be reached by train from any major European city, although there are no direct trains from the UK; options include travelling via Paris to Munich and then on to Budapest or via Dover to Ostend and Vienna (either way, the journey time is at least 24 hours). Check uk.voyages-sncf.com for details. Unless you are aged under 26 or over 60, it's an expensive (though more environmentally friendly and often very scenic) option.

The following international rail passes are valid in Hungary: InterRail (www.interrail.eu), EurailPass (and its variants; www.eurail.com) and Hungarian FlexiPass for students (www.isecard.com). Budapest has three international railway stations, **Keleti**, **Nyugati** and **Déli** (all have metro stations attached).

By car/coach. Budapest is connected by major motorways to Berlin, Prague and Vienna. It has long been held that the cheapest way to get from London to Budapest is by coach, although with the advent of budget airlines, that may no longer be the case. The bus journey takes some 31 hours and may not be much fun in summer, as buses can get crowded. See www.eurolines.com for details. Long-haul buses arrive at Népliget Coach Station (Üllői út 131).

If you plan to drive across the continent, the most direct route is via Ostend, Brussels, Cologne, Frankfurt, Linz and Vienna. Budapest is about 1730km (1080 miles) from London.

GUIDES AND TOURS

There are numerous guided tours in Budapest: **Cityrama** (tel: 302-4382; www.cityrama.hu); **Budatours** (www.budatours.hu); **Program Centrum** (www.programcentrum.hu) and **IBUSZ** (www.ibusz.hu) offer a range of services.

Tours are available to the Danube Bend, the Puszta, and Lake Balaton; as are special interest tours (health and wellness, seasonal customs and folklore, etc).

Mahart Passnave (www.mahartpassnave.hu) and **Legenda KFTs** (www.legenda.hu) are perhaps the most established operators offering Danube boat trips. The shortest of the cruises are hour-long sightseeing tours with commentary in various languages. In the summer, day trips are available taking passengers up the Danube Bend to the historic towns of Esztergom, Szentendre and Visegrád. There are also evening cruises with buffet suppers, music and dancing.

You can also go sightseeing in Budapest by helicopter, light aircraft or hot-air balloon. Hotel reception areas have brochures about excursions and Tourinform can also help.

Walking tours of special interest include those by **Absolute Walking Tours** (www.absolutetours.com). **Budapest City Tour** (www.budapestcitytour.com) organizes tours of Jewish Budapest. In addition, it can also arrange private tours, tailored to your requirements.

Yellow Zebra Bike Tours (tel: 565-6115; www.yellowzebrabikes.com) organizes bicycle, e-bike and segway tours.

H

HEALTH AND MEDICAL CARE

Hungarian doctors and healthcare professionals are highly skilled, and most speak English and German. The Hungarian National Health Service is well equipped to handle emergencies and there are reciprocal arrangements for citizens of the EEA (European Economic Area), which includes the EU member countries plus Norway, Iceland and Liechtenstein. Emergency treatment is free for foreigners; all other treatment has to be paid for when you receive the service. EU residents should obtain the European Health Insurance Card (EHIC), which entitles them to medical and hospital treatment free of charge; UK citizens should note that when their current EHIC expires, it will be replaced by the GHIC (Global Health Insurance Card).

The American **First Med Center** is located in Buda (Hattyú utca 14; tel: 224-9090; www.firstmedcenters.com).

Tap water is drinkable, but don't drink anything marked *nem ivóviz*, which means non-drinkable.

Pharmacies. Look for the sign *gyógyszertár* or *patika*. Chemists only sell pharmaceutical and related products; for cosmetics and toiletries you will need an *illatszerbolt* or *drogéria*; for photo supplies a *fotószaküzlet*. One of the night pharmacies is **Teréz Patika** (VI Teréz körút 41; tel: 311-4439; www.terezpatika.hu).

Where's the nearest pharmacy? **Hol a legközelebbi patika?**
I need a doctor/dentist. **Orvosra/Fogorvosra van szük ségem.**

HOLIDAYS *(hivatalos ünnep)*
1 January New Year's Day
15 March National Holiday Anniversary of 1848 Revolution
April Easter Monday
1 May Labour Day
June Pentecost
20 August St Stephen's Day
23 October Remembrance (Republic) Day
25 December Christmas Day
26 December Boxing Day

I

INTERNET

Hotels, shopping malls, restaurants and cafés offer free wi-fi access, which is also available at the airport and on some squares. See www.wificafespots.com for a map of the city's wi-fi access spots. There are also several internet cafés. Vist@ NetCafe (Váci út 6; tel: 70 585 3924; www.vistanetcafe.com) in the very centre of the city has long hours, and you can also scan and print your documents there.

L

LANGUAGE

Hungarian is the mother tongue of 95 percent of the population. It is wholly unrelated to the languages of the surrounding countries and is classified in the Finno-Ugric family of languages. It is notoriously difficult and continues to baffle linguists. The majority of Budapestis speak German, and many, especially the young, speak English fluently.

One source of confusion is how to address a Hungarian. The surname always precedes the Christian name; Western Europeans would say or write Károly Jókai, whereas Hungarians say Jókai Károly. Second, there is no direct equivalent of Mr or Mrs; the nearest terms, which are very formal, are *Uram* for Mr and *Hölgyem* for Mrs.

LEFT LUGGAGE

There are facilities at the three main railway stations and at the Central Bus Station.

LGBTQ+ TRAVELLERS

Budapest is generally safe and welcoming to LGBTQ+ people. In many ways, however, Hungary feels a little behind its European neighbours when it comes to acceptance of its queer communities, and it doesn't have a particular gay area skin to London's Soho or the Marais in Paris. While there is an active LGBTQ+ community in Budapest and an enthusiastic Pride parade every year, same-sex love is still viewed with suspicion by some, and public displays of affection are not the norm for queer or straight couples. The main LGBTQ+ support organization in Hungary is the **Háttér Society** (tel: 329-2670; www. hatter.hu). **CoXx Men's Bar** (VIII Dohány utca 38; www.coxx.hu) is a popular gay venue in Budapest.

Good morning **Jó reggelt**
Good afternoon **Jó napot**
Hi (informal, singular/plural) **Szia/Sziasztok**
Goodnight **Jó éjszakát**
Goodbye **Viszontlátásra**
Good day (formal) **Tó napot**
Thank you **Köszönöm**
Do you speak English/French/German? **Beszél angolul/ franciául/németül?**
Yes/no **igen/nem**
please **kérem**
pull/push **húzni/tolni**
open **nyitva**
closed **zárva**
entrance **bejárat**
exit **kijárat**
road **út**
street **utca**
square **tér**
boulevard **körút**
bridge **híd**
pharmacy **gyógyszertár**
post office **posta**
railway station **pályaudvar**

shop **bolt/üzlet**
department store **áruház**
How much is this? **Ez mennyibe kerül?**
Where is the nearest police station? **Hol van a legközelebbi rendőrség?**

M

MAPS

Ibusz offices supply visitors with free maps of the city that are sufficient for most purposes. If you want a more comprehensive map, look for the *Cartographia Budapest City* or *Budapest Atlas* maps of Budapest, available in most bookstores.

MEDIA

Newspapers and magazines. *Budapest Business Journal* (www.bbj.hu) is the English-language weekly newspaper in the city. Major European and US newspapers usually arrive on the day of publication, although some are a day late.
Television. All hotels rated 4-star and above, and some 3-star, offer satellite television in rooms.

MONEY

Currency. The unit of currency is the forint (HUF). Coins in circulation are HUF 1, 2, 5, 10, 20, 50, 100 and 200. Banknotes are in denominations of HUF 100, 200, 500, 1,000, 2,000, 5,000, 10,000 and 20,000. Most places also accept euro.
Foreign exchange offices. These are found in banks, hotels, larger camp-sites, travel agents and large shops, but some offer exchange rates as much as 20 percent lower than banks, which always offer the most advantageous rates. There isn't a black market any more, so if you are accosted and offered money-changing opportunities, steer clear. It's good to have a few

dollars, euros or pounds for emergencies, and you may get a better rate of exchange for cash.

Credit and debit cards. Visa, MasterCard and AmEx are frequently accepted in hotels, restaurants and large shops (look for the logos). Since the pandemic, cards are more widely accepted than ever; be aware, though, that some supermarkets, museums and railway stations may ask for payments in cash. Post offices (there are more than 3200 of them) will dispense cash on production of your card.

ATMs. Cash machines are widespread and most major cards are accepted. They dispense HUFs. However, there are also two ATMs in the centre of Budapest that dispense euros: in Deák Ferenc utca 5–7 and Babér utca 9.

O

OPENING HOURS

Most businesses in Budapest are open Mon–Fri 8am–5pm. **Shopping centres** tend to be open Mon–Sat 10am–9pm, Sun 10am–6pm. Smaller **shops** are open Mon–Fri 9 or 10am–6 or 7pm, Sat 9 or 10am–1 or 2pm, but some close all day Saturday. For 24-hour shopping look for the sign 'Non-Stop'. **Banks** open Mon–Fri 8am–3pm, although some close at 1pm on Friday. **Museums** mostly open Tues–Sun 10am–6pm, and be aware that many tourist attractions are shut on Mondays. **Post** offices open Mon–Fri 8am–6pm, Sat 8am–1pm.

P

POLICE

Police (*rendőrség*) wear blue-and-grey uniforms. Traffic police also wear white caps and white leather to make them more visible. During July and August, tourist police with translators patrol the streets.

Police: tel: 107
Budapest Police Headquarters: tel: 343-0034

POST OFFICES

Post offices (Magyar Posta) handle mail, telephones, telegraphs, telex and (at the larger offices) fax. Stamps (*bélyeg*) are best bought at tobacconists or where postcards are sold. Most hotels will stamp and post your mail for you. Post boxes are painted red. The majority of post offices open Mon–Fri 8am–6pm, Sat 8am–1pm.

I'd like a stamp for this letter/postcard please. **Kérek egy bélyeget erre a levélre/a képeslapra.**

PUBLIC TRANSPORT

The Budapest Transport Authority (BKV) operates an extensive system with four metro lines, blue local buses, yellow trams and red trolley-buses. You must buy a ticket before boarding. They are sold at stations, travel bureaux and tobacconists. If you are staying for several days, it makes sense to buy a three- or seven-day travel card. Current fares and additional information are available at www.bkv.hu.

Most public transport runs between 4.30am and 11pm. There is a limited number of night buses and trams (look for the suffix é on their number). Don't forget to validate your ticket by punching it in the red machine (passes don't need validating), which are located on board buses and trams, and at the entrance to metro stations. BKV ticket inspectors, wearing red armbands, patrol public transport frequently and levy fare dodgers with on-the-spot fines.

Buses. A bus (*busz*) stop is marked by a blue-bordered rectangular sign with the letter M and a list of stops on the route.

Trams. Yellow trams (*villamos*), usually of three to four carriages, cover a 190km (120-mile) network; some run throughout the night.

Taxis. Budapest's taxi drivers are notorious for overcharging foreigners, and unless you're laden with luggage or have some other reason for not travelling on public transport, they should be avoided. If, however, you do want a taxi, call one of the following firms: **Citytaxi** (tel: 211-1111; www.citytaxi.hu), **Fő Taxi** (tel: 222-2222; www.fotaxi.hu) or **Taxi4** (tel: 444-4444; www.taxi4.hu). Hailing a cab on the street is not recommended, but if you do so, always find out the rate and make sure the meter is working (and set at zero before you set off), or agree on the fare in advance. Otherwise, you can download the Bolt app (www.bolt.eu) on your smartphone to order a ride.

Metro. There are two interchange stops between the metro's four lines: at Deák tér station and at Kálvin Tér. Remember to validate your ticket before you get on the metro; the validating machines stamp the starting time of your trip onto your ticket. A single trip costs HUF 350, and HUF 450 when bought on board. You can also buy a block of 10 tickets (HUF 3000).

Trains. There are four hév suburban commuter lines: to Szentendre, Gödöllö (with a branch line to Csömör), Csepel and Ráckeve. Szentendre (via Aquincum) is reached via Batthyány tér station and Gödöllö is reached from Örs vezér tere. If you have a travel card, you pay only for the stretch outside Budapest city limits. Inter-city trains operate from three Budapest stations: **Keleti** (Baross tér; most international trains), **Nyugati** (Nyugati tér; mostly destinations east) and **Déli** (Alkotás út).

The main **railway ticket office** for national and international trains is located at Andrássy út 73–5 (Máv; tel: 349-4949; www.mav.hu).

A special treat for railway enthusiasts are the **nostalgia trains**, vintage and steam locomotives run by máv Nosztalgia (ticket office at Teréz krt. 55; tel: 269-5242; www.mavcsoport.hu) that trundle to the Gödöllö Palace, the Hungarian Plain, Danube Bend and Eger. The Royal Hungarian Express visits the cities of the old Austro-Hungarian Empire (Prague and Vienna).

River transport. In the summer season, the Budapest Transport Authority operates a boat service between Rómaifürdö, Batthyány tér, Szent Gellért tér and Haller utca. Pleasure boats run to and from the Danube Bend, hydrofoils also run to Esztergom and Vienna (Mahart Pass Nave; tel: 484-4013; www.mahartpassnave.hu).

R

RELIGION

The majority of Hungarians are Roman Catholics. Mass is usually said in Hungarian, but in some churches, it is said in Latin, English or German. Other denominations and faiths, notably Protestant, Eastern Orthodox and Jewish, are also represented. There is a small Muslim community.

T

TELEPHONES

You can roam on one of three Hungarian mobile networks or buy a local SIM card. The mobile network operators are: Magyar Telekom (www.telekom.hu), Yettel (www.yettel.hu) and Vodafone (www.vodafone.hu).

To make an international call from a public phone, dial the international access code (00), followed by the country code and the telephone number, including the area code. There are no off-peak rates. For national calls beyond Budapest, dial the national access code (06), followed by the area code and number. A local call within Budapest has 7 digits; it is not necessary to dial the area code. Mobile telephone numbers have 11 digits. The network is being modernized, so numbers change frequently. If the number has changed, there's a message in Hungarian followed by one in English (so don't hang up) giving the new number. For international directory assistance, tel: 199.

TIME ZONES

Hungary follows Central European Time (Greenwich Mean Time +1 hour, or US Eastern Standard Time +6 hours). In summer, the clock is put one hour ahead (GMT +2).

TIPPING

Tipping is the norm in Hungary. It is customary to leave 10 percent at restaurants and round up the bill in bars. Some restaurants may add a 10 percent service charge to the bill, so look carefully and ask, if this appears to be the case, so that you avoid tipping twice.

Porters, housekeeping at hotels, toilet attendants, violinists playing at your table, massage therapists at thermal baths and tourist guides also expect tips; be aware, this is their livelihood.

TOILETS

In Budapest all public toilets are pay toilets. Cafés will usually admit patrons for free on production of a receipt for what they have consumed on the premises.

For men's toilets, look out for the word *Férfiak* or, more commonly, *férfi* (occasionally *urak*). For women, look for *Nők* or (again, more commonly) *női* (and occasionally *hólgyek*).

TOURIST INFORMATION

The **Tourism Office of Budapest** operates tourist information points at Deák Ferenc tér, Sütő utca 2 and Heroes' Square, Olof Palme sétány 5, and it has branches at both terminals of the Budapest Airport (www.budapestinfo.hu and www.tourinform.hu). A **tourist information hotline** is maintained on tel: 438-8080 (daily 8am–8pm).

Ibusz (www.ibusz.hu) is a major tour operator, providing a booking service and organizing excursions.

W

WEBSITES

The following websites may be useful:

www.budapest.com
www.budapestinfo.hu
www.bestofbudapest.com
www.gotohungary.com
www.tourinform.hu
www.visithungary.com

Y

YOUTH HOSTELS

There are numerous hostels *(Ifjúsági szállás)* in Budapest. Avoid the touts at the railway station offering hostel accommodation; they will send you to somewhere expensive in the back of beyond. The International Youth Hostels Federation can be accessed at www.hihostels.com. You can also pick up a list of addresses at Budapest tourist information points.

WHERE TO STAY

Hotels in Hungary are graded from one to five stars. Budapest's standard visitor accommodation has improved dramatically in the years since the iron curtain came down. As well as quality, the city now has quantity too, which for most of the year keeps prices at a very reasonable level. It is wise, however, to book ahead, particularly for September, New Year, Easter, and at the turn of July and August, when the Hungarian Grand Prix is staged. High season on Lake Balaton is from Easter to September, and during peak times demand is such that some establishments offer half-board only.

The following guide denotes the rack rate price of a double room with bath/shower in high season (May to October, and Christmas) including breakfast and VAT. Hotel room rates, especially at the upper end, are usually quoted in euros, though some are given in US dollars.

€€€€€	**over 250 euros**
€€€€	**200–250 euros**
€€€	**150–200 euros**
€€	**100–150 euros**
€	**less than 100 euros**

BUDA

Aquincum €€€€ *III Árpád Fejedlem útja 94, tel: 436-4100,* www.aquincum hotel.com. Located near the Árpád Bridge, this is a modern, luxury, thermal-bath hotel with full spa and balneotherapy facilities. Inside, you'll find attractive restaurants and bars and even an executive club for business travellers. Importantly, the hotel also has wheelchair access.

Baltazár Budapest €€€€ *I Országház utca 31, tel: 300-7051,* http://baltazar budapest.com. A family-owned boutique hotel in the heart of the Old Town. Rooms have been individually designed and feature contemporary artwork and graphics juxtaposed with vintage furniture. There is also *Baltazár Grill* serving a menu of Hungarian and international dishes as well as an intimate bar lined by a selection of 300 wines, mostly from the Carpathian Basin. Remarkably attentive staff.

Buda Castle Fashion Hotel €€€€ | *Úri utca 39, tel: 225-3878,* www.buda castlehotelbudapest.com. Located in a fifteenth-century townhouse, this is a fully equipped modern, four-star hotel with 25 rooms. The interior design is sophisticated and stylish, yet still cosy. Major Buda sights are within easy walking distance.

Exe Carlton Hotel €€ | *Apor Péter utca 3, tel: 224-0999,* www.eurostarshotels. com. A down-to-earth, fairly modern building at the foot of Fisherman's Bastion in a quiet alleyway. Simply (but warmly) furnished and very clean. Some rooms have balconies, and many upper rooms have great views. Healthy buffet breakfasts. Within walking distance of Buda Castle and Széchenyi Baths.

Hilton Budapest €€€€€ *Hess András tér 1–3, tel: 889-6600,* www.hilton. com. One of the most famous – and owing to its architecture – most notorious hotels in town. You'll either love or hate the modern hotel's incorporation of a thirteenth-century Dominican church into its design. Rooms are fairly cookie-cutter in style, though comfortable; the best come with fine city and river views. The extensive facilities include a business centre and casino. The *Icon* restaurant's panoramic windows overlook Fisherman's Bastion and the Parliament. On the menu you'll find both light, healthy meals and dishes that are sheer indulgence. Wheelchair access. 322 rooms.

Lánchíd 19 €€€€ | *Lánchíd utca 19, tel: 419-1900,* www.lanchid19hotel. hu. This bright and stylish boutique hotel occupies an enviable location, just a few steps away from the funicular up to the Castle District and the Chain Bridge across to Pest. The building is designed with glass panels arranged in waves on its facade, which changes colour according to the season. Look closer and you can see fish and other river life etched in patterns on the glass. Inside, the attention to detail is similarly impressive, with artworks by Françoise Gilot (one of Picasso's wives), designer furniture and sleek bathrooms. The three suites at the top of the building have whirlpool baths from which you can enjoy panoramic views of the city through enormous picture windows. The hotel has its own restaurant, which serves dishes expertly cooked in a modern international style. 48 rooms.

Maison €€ *Országház utca 17, tel: 405-4980,* www.maisonbudapest.hu. Once a bakery, this boutique hotel at the northern end of the Castle is a welcome addition to the area. Some of its rooms have whirlpool bathtubs, and all have tasteful, if whimsical, decor – think exposed brick and ceiling beams and wooden floors. The rooms are collected around a pleasant courtyard where you can sit outside in warm weather.

Novotel Budapest City €€ *XII Alkotás utca 63–67, tel: 372-5400,* www.novotel-bud-congress.hu. Unpretentious, modern hotel in a park area, surrounded by spreading chestnut trees. No-frills rooms are simply furnished and clean. It's next door to the Budapest Convention Centre, so handy for events there. There's a restaurant, indoor pool, tennis court, hammam, terrace and gym.

Park Plaza Budapest €€€ / *Bem rakpart 16–19, tel: 487-9487,* www.artotels.com. This boutique hotel is styled by Donald Sultan, the American contemporary artist, and it displays 600 of his works. The hotel is spread across four Baroque townhouses beside the Danube, opposite Parliament. It's a hip lifestyle hotel with a good restaurant, the *Chelsea*, serving light, tasty meals. Wheelchair access.

St. George Residence €€€€ / *Fortuna utca 4, tel: 393-5700,* www.stgeorgehotel.hu. Located in a reconstructed Baroque townhouse dating back to fourteenth century, this hotel brims with exquisite charm. The rooms are elegant with stylish antique furnishings. There are standard, superior and executive suites, as well as a formal restaurant with cathedral ceilings and a rather retro smoking lounge.

Hotel Victoria €€ / *Bem rakpart 11, tel: 457-8080,* www.victoria.hu. This small, modern hotel gazes out across the Danube on the Buda side. The rooms are spacious, and the service is efficient and friendly. High-speed internet connection is available and there are laptops for hire. The price is excellent for the location, within a 15-minute walk of Buda Castle.

MARGARET ISLAND

Ensana Grand Margaret Island Health Spa Hotel €€€ *XIII Margitsziget, tel: 889-4700,* www.ensanahotels.com/en/hotels/grand-margaret-island. The grande dame of the island was built in 1893 in a Neoclassical style, and rather magically, is linked by an underground tunnel to a neighbouring spa. By contrast to the hotel, the spa was built in the Brutalist concrete style popular in communist countries at the time. As well as an idyllic location, the hotel offers therapy for locomotive disorders, dentistry, cardiac and cosmetic surgery and a large range of health and beauty services. Naturally, there is provision for travellers with disabilities.

PEST

Amadeus Apartments € *various locations in Pest, tel: 30 942-2893,* www.amadeus.hu. Independent, fully equipped apartments, mostly in Pest, but also in Buda, ideal for those who like to come and go as they please and cook their own meals. Two-room boltholes, each with bath, toilet and kitchen facilities, accommodate 1–4 people in short-term lets.

Anantara Budapest €€€€€ *V Erzsébet körút 9–11, tel: 886-6111,* www.boscolohotels.com. The *Anantara* occupies one of the most beautiful and extraordinary buildings in the city, the New York Palace. Originally built as an insurance company's headquarters in the late nineteenth century (Budapest's heyday), it was designed in a flamboyant neo-Baroque style, with ornate interiors and sumptuous fittings. Luxury, comfort and attention to detail are in abundance throughout. Facilities include a spa, cigar bar, business centre and restaurant. The hotel is also famed for its *New York Café*, where you can take high tea in the grand style surrounded by plush furnishings and attentive waiters.

Budapest Marriott €€€€€ *V Apáczai Csere János utca 4, tel: 486-5000,* www.marriott.com/budhu. A five-star city centre hotel on the banks of the Danube. Every luxuriously appointed room enjoys splendid views of Castle Hill and many have small balconies. Friendly and efficient service and excellent facilities, including business and fitness centres. Wheelchair access.

Budapest Panorama Central € *V Károly Körút 10, tel: 328-0870,* www.buda
pestpanoramacentral.com. Decent budget hotel in the centre of Pest, close
to the Great Synagogue and other major sights, metro station and tram
stops. Air-conditioned comfortable rooms and cooking facilities for guests.
Good value for money.

Danubius Hotel Astoria €€€ *V Kossuth Lajos utca 19–21, tel: 889-6000,* www.
danubiushotels.com. Staying at the *Astoria* is like being plonked in a film set.
It has tradition and style, with mirrors, chandeliers and carpets that evoke
the ambience of the Belle Epoque. It was given the name when it opened
in 1914 by the first manager, who had been at the *Waldorf Astoria* in New
York. It's been updated since, and is still a fine hotel. The *Café Astoria and
Restaurant* serves fine, classic Hungarian fare and is also worth a visit for the
glittering decor.

Gerlóczy Boutique Hotel €€ *Gerlóczy utca 1, tel: 501-4000,* www.gerloczy.
com. Above the café of the same name, the nineteen elegant *Gerlóczy* rooms
all lead off a spiral staircase topped by a coloured glass skylight. The rooms
are colour themed according to floor (grey, blue, red and yellow-green from
the ground upwards), though all have similar fixtures and fittings: high doors
and ceilings, parquet flooring and gorgeous, brass-fitted bathrooms, some
with clawfoot tubs, others with showers only. Two rooms have small balconies looking out over the square. One of the best value-for-money places in
the city, especially if you can nab a slightly cheaper attic room.

K+K Hotel Opera €€€ *V Révay utca 24, tel: 269-0222,* www.kkhotels.com. A
branch of the reliable Austrian chain, this hotel is located conveniently for
the opera house and the theatre district. The interior is stylishly designed,
and facilities include a gym and underground parking.

Kempinski Hotel Corvinus €€€€€ *V Erzsébet tér 7–8, tel: 429-3777,* www.
kempinski.com/en/budapest/hotel-corvinus. Architecturally striking building infused with a great sense of style, elegance and flair, and luxurious
rooms and suites that have earned the hotel its five-star rating. There's an
informal *ÉS Bistró* and contemporary *Nobu* restaurant serving Japanese cuisine. Facilities include an indoor swimming pool, fitness centre and boutique
shop. Wheelchair access.

Lavender Circus € *Múzeum körút 37, tel: 417-7763*, www.lavendercircus. com. Situated opposite the Hungarian National Museum, this eccentric little haunt has a very individual touch: the owner Ádám has designed all the rooms himself – expect vintage furniture, goldfish tanks and satirical artwork gracing the walls. The pricier rooms on the second floor have en-suite bathrooms and kitchenettes. The reception is on the third floor, and there is no lift. You can also book one of three apartments behind the Opera House.

Mamaison Hotel Andrássy €€€€ *VI Andrássy út 111, tel: 462-2100*, www. mamaison.com. This four-star boutique hotel occupies a 1930s Bauhaus-inspired building designed by Alfréd Hajós, not far from Heroes' Square. The rooms are luxuriously appointed, and the best ones have grand four-poster beds. The in-house restaurant is the reputable *La Perle Noire*, which ensures that breakfast is a pleasurable experience. Guests at the *Mamaison Andrássy* can also use the sauna and fitness centre of its sister hotel in the city, at Izabella utca 61.

Marmara Hotel €€ *V Nagy Ignác utca 21, tel: 501-9100*, www.marmara.hu. This city-centre boutique hotel is newly built and has been designed with great attention to detail. It seems that every surface has been upholstered or covered in some plush finish, and the warm but restrained colours of the decor enhance the feeling of comfort and calm.

Medosz Hotel € *VI Jókai tér 9, tel: 374-3000*, www.medoszhotel.hu. A big hotel in the vicinity of Oktogon metro station and right across lively Liszt Ferenc tér, which is lined with popular restaurants. Rooms are not fancy, but they are clean, comfortable and spacious. Some of them overlook Andrássy út. There's an excellent buffet breakfast, and helpful reception.

Ritz-Carlton Budapest €€€€€ *V Erzsébet tér 9–10, tel: 429-5500*, www.ritz carlton.com. There are eight grades of luxurious rooms and suites in this five-star hotel, all handsomely furnished and finished to a high standard. Public rooms glitter with chandeliers. The posh restaurant, *Kupola Lounge*, serves food fit for royalty beneath a regal Art Deco glass dome. The facilities are excellent: there is a swimming pool, a fitness centre and tennis courts. Wheelchair access.

INDEX

THE MINI ROUGH GUIDE TO
BUDAPEST

First Edition 2023

Editor: Joanna Reeves
Author: Paul Murphy
Updater: Annie Warren
Picture Editor: Tom Smyth
Cartography Update: Katie Bennett
Layout: Grzegorz Madejak
Head of DTP and Pre-Press: Rebeka Davies
Head of Publishing: Sarah Clark
Photography Credits: 123RF 91;
budapestinfo.hu 4CL; Fotolia 71; iStock 21, 26,
35, 79, 81, 83, 98; Labyrinth of Buda Castle 36;
Ming Tang-Evans/Apa Publications 6T, 6B, 7B,
7T, 17, 29, 33, 38, 41, 42, 44, 46, 49, 50, 52, 54,
55, 57, 58, 60, 63, 67, 68, 69, 72/73, 75, 77, 84,
86, 89, 92, 95, 99, 101, 103; Neil Schlecht/Apa
Publications 64; Public domain15; Shutterstock
1, 4BL, 4TL, 4TC, 4TR, 4BR, 4CR, 5C, 5B, 5T, 11,
13, 18, 22, 24, 30
Cover Credits: Hungarian Parliament on the
Danube **Botond Horvath/Shutterstock**

Distribution

UK, Ireland and Europe: Apa Publications (UK)
Ltd; sales@roughguides.com
United States and Canada: Ingram Publisher
Services; ips@ingramcontent.com
Australia and New Zealand: Booktopia;
retailer@booktopia.com.au
Worldwide: Apa Publications (UK) Ltd;
sales@roughguides.com

**Special Sales, Content Licensing
and CoPublishing**
Rough Guides can be purchased in bulk
quantities at discounted prices. We can create
special editions, personalised jackets and
corporate imprints tailored to your needs.
sales@roughguides.com; http://roughguides.com

Printed in Czech Republic

This book was produced using **Typefi** automated
publishing software.

Contact us
Every effort has been made to provide accurate
information in this publication, but changes
are inevitable. The publisher cannot be held
responsible for any resulting loss, inconvenience
or injury sustained by any traveller as a result of
information or advice contained in the guide.
We would appreciate it if readers would call our
attention to any errors or outdated information, or if
you feel we've left something out. Please send your
comments with the subject line "Rough Guide Mini
Budapest Update" to mail@uk.roughguides.com.

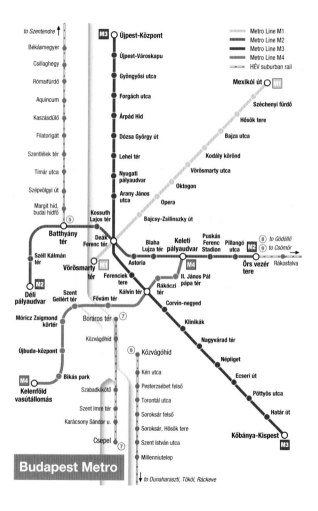

Budapest Metro